JUL 0 6 2011

ALSO BY CRAIG HOVEY

The Way of the Cockroach

The

ACCOUNTANT'S
GUIDE

to the

UNIVERSE

CONTENTS

The
ACCOUNTANT'S
GUIDE
to the
UNIVERSE

Heaven and Hell by the Numbers

CRAIG HOVEY

Thomas Dunne Books
St. Martin's Press ☙ New York

657
HOV

THOMAS DUNNE BOOKS.
An imprint of St. Martin's Press.

THE ACCOUNTANT'S GUIDE TO THE UNIVERSE. Copyright © 2010 by Craig Hovey.
All rights reserved. Printed in the United States of America. For information,
address St. Martin's Press, 175 Fifth Avenue, New York, N.Y. 10010.

www.thomasdunnebooks.com
www.stmartins.com

Design by Susan Walsh

ISBN 978-0-312-37624-6

FIRST EDITION: November 2010

10 9 8 7 6 5 4 3 2 1

This book is dedicated to
Dr. Alec Sutherland,
the greatest English professor
in the observable universe and beyond.

The

ACCOUNTANT'S
GUIDE

to the

UNIVERSE

One

THE OUTSOURCING OF HEAVEN AND HELL

First you learn to measure with dollars. Then you gain the sense to account for eternity.

Accounting's rise to eternal prominence began soon after God outsourced Heaven and Hell to AudiTrix. AudiTrix is a huge conglomerate headquartered in the Triangulum Galaxy and their operations span the universe. Since AudiTrix did not have God's all-knowing power, it was vital that it develop a sound process for deciding who went where in the afterlife. Eternity is forever, after all, and that leaves little margin for error.

IN THE BEGINNING

In the early days of its Heaven and Hell operations AudiTrix addressed the new venture by organizing judgment councils of Supreme Counters. Nine members constituted each council and they were charged with reviewing the life events of recently deceased subjects. Their task was three-part: first, to total and weight all the good things judges had done in life, with "good" defined as actions that added value to the world they inhabited; second, to total and weight all the bad things judges had done in life, with "bad" defined as actions that detracted from the value of their worlds; and third, to subtract the total value of the bad from the total value of the good to arrive at a net score. Then, all the Supreme Counters' net scores were added together and divided by nine. This yielded a number that, in the early days, came to be known as the Final Result of the Wise Nine, or FROWN, Index. A positive FROWN meant that the judgee before them had left the world a better place and Heaven would be the final destination. The higher the index score, the loftier the heavenly perch. A negative FROWN meant that the judgee had left the world in worse shape and Hell became the final destination. The depth and heat of the eternal divot was determined by how low the index had been driven.

AudiTrix provided Supreme Counters with extensive Life Event Assessment and Calculation training. The counters themselves were chosen from almost every walk of life, with the common requirement being that all were wise, mature beings with vetted histories of sound and fair conduct. It seemed reasonable to assume that nine such council members could be depended on to arrive at fair and balanced majority decisions with regularity.

Before long, however, it became apparent that no amount of LEAC training or reasoned debate could prevent irregularity. Personal opinions, lapses of judgment, grudges and vendettas, outside pressures, and outright corruption (Supreme Counters were not well paid) plagued the process. Many an innocent received a one-way ticket to Hell and plenty of evildoers found their way into Heaven on the heels of 5-4 split decisions.

God saw this, and he was not pleased. Before long his patience wore thin and AudiTrix received a wrathful Lightning Bolt Express message commanding it to suspend operations immediately. AudiTrix had forty days and forty nights to prepare and present a dramatically better approach for God's approval.

FROM THE MOUTHS OF BARBARIANS

What AudiTrix needed to find in a hurry was a simple, fair, and objective system with principles so clearly spelled out that all room for creative application and abuse was removed. Any being facing judgment in any time or place had to know that the rules would lead to the same decision, regardless of whether best friend or worst enemy administered the judgment mechanism. Determined not to lose its divine contract and face universal scorn and ridicule, AudiTrix threw itself into scouring galaxies near and far for ideas and inspiration. No solar system was left unturned and envoys were dispatched to every planet where intelligent life had taken root.

Earth barely made the cut, but it was there that AudiTrix's desperate search met with astounding success.

Twelve thousand years earlier a group of AudiTrix executives had visited Earth on a corporate team-building exercise that required them to negotiate the rigors of a primitive environment. The idea was to help them improve their skills at dealing with difficult customers. They found Earth to be a hostile planet whose populations were mired in shockingly backward states of existence. Its most advanced species, human beings, were organized in small bands of hunter-gatherers barely able to feed, clothe, or shelter themselves. They were completely unable to get along with anybody outside their familial clans and regarded all who strayed into their territories as instant enemies.

Before the AudiTrix executives had a chance to bond with each other and begin banging on their assigned drums, a swarm of spear-wielding Neanderthals with murder on their minds mistook the strange looking back-slapping creatures for a new food source and attacked. With their training mission ending in a bloody disaster, all undigested AudiTrix personnel fled Earth and swore never to return—though the planet continued to receive upper-management support as a perfect training site for heel-nipping youngsters rising up through the ranks too rapidly.

Despite this earlier sordid episode, a few brave envoys decided to make a side trip to Earth after an excursion to a more promising nearby planet, Neptune, bore no fruit. What they found stunned them. In a mere twelve thousand years humans had organized themselves into economies of incredible complexity, breadth, and efficiency where the surest path to wealth required all members to trade their limited resources with each other in ways that benefited every party to the exchange. So successful did the process prove to be that life spans had tripled since the last AudiTrix visit and living standards were even more dramatically improved. All of this occurred in an interval that is a mere flash in terms of evolutionary time.

For AudiTrix's purposes it was not human progress itself that caught its devoted attention but the mechanism employed for tracking and evaluating it. This system followed deceptively simple rules, making it possible for any entity to document everything he or she owned, earned, owed, used up, and had left over after all the bills were paid. It measured the valuable limited resources sacrificed and all resources gained in return, and then clearly stated the difference between the two as a profit or loss. Standard units of measure were used to generate the numbers, and all those viewing them agreed on their values.

Not only were all inflows and outflows of resources recorded; each transaction consisted of increases and decreases in various accounts that always balanced out, with no exceptions. Whether for the smallest concern or the largest enterprise, when the accounting system's transactions were totaled, the scales of value were equal on either side, even if they were made up of millions or billions of exchanges per day. Clear rules existed to guide operations and numerous provisions were in place to dictate responsibilities for insiders and outsiders alike, making sure that the rules were being obeyed.

The method employed on Earth was called *accounting,* a name AudiTrix retained, along with the basic rules and spirit of the discipline itself. What amazed observers most was that humans, formerly known as the most violent, suspicious, and antisocial species on Earth or any other planet, had devised an information system that showed them how much better or worse off their pursuits made them and provided irrefutable evidence that cooperating with others brought great benefits. The invention and implementation of accounting did for humans what millions of years' worth of evolution could not.

AudiTrix said to its corporate self, "If accounting can do this much for savages, imagine how well it will work for the civilized portions of the universe!" AudiTrix envoys multiplied and quickly spread out over the face of the Earth to gather up every piece of information on the discipline they could find, and then uploaded it to corporate headquarters.

At the end of forty days and forty nights AudiTrix made its presentation. God saw that earthly accounting was good and had the potential to be fitted to the purposes of Heaven and Hell. But before allowing it to be fruitful and multiply throughout the universe, God decreed that AudiTrix first use Earth as an exclusive field-test site, where it could observe accounting boldly going where no bean counting had gone before.

If accounting could make it there, accounting could make it anywhere.

Two

FORBIDDEN FRUIT

To err is human; to profit is divine.

Mastering accounting is like learning how to speak a new language. On Earth accounting is called the "language of business," but in a more universal sense it is the language of choice. Accounting as practiced in the earthly business realm uses currency to record the actions of individuals and firms and then goes on to document how well or how poorly the decisions they made pay off in the future.

This framework, AudiTrix concluded, could be expanded to assess the conduct of individuals in the course of living their lives. Dollars and cents cannot be used for this broader application, of course, which is why karma koins were invented. Before their workings can be fathomed, though, it is necessary to understand the basics of standard-issue accounting, as practiced from the wilds of Wall Street to the shops on Main Street.

After their proposal for revising and redeploying the Heaven and Hell operation was conditionally accepted, the counters at AudiTrix developed a rigorous training program to teach this new language to fresh recruits and ensure that they gained a high level of fluency in it. Recruits successfully completing their training were no longer simply told to go forth and judge; instead, their competence was tested with a grueling two-day examination. Those who sat for it successfully were certified to become practitioners of the eternal accounting art and given the HAP designation to put after their names. This identified them as "heavenly auditing professionals," that is, professionals of the highest order. AudiTrix then created a corporate slogan to accompany the new credential: "Nobody shall be HAP-less on Judgment Day."

Becoming a HAP entails mastering traditional accounting and demonstrating the ability to apply its concepts to the much harder to measure realms of human intention, action, and result. Merely recording that which is easiest to measure does not yield an accurate valuation of firms or individuals. Intangibles must be considered, such as quality of life, contributions made to the present and future well-being of others, and what people are able to make of the differing amounts of resources they are given at the starting line.

FROM THE PENDULUM INTO THE PIT

I, your author, am among those who were judged and sent to Hell by AudiTrix before it made the switch to earthly accounting, in the days when easily observable actions were all that counted. Though I never quarreled with the interpretations of the negative things I was caught doing on eternal tape—this would have been stupid because it does not lie—there is another side to me that was ignored (and is admittedly harder to locate). To conduct a true accounting, all transactions have to be included: the good, the bad, the ugly, and the unexpected. Along with many other dwellers in the universe's hottest cellar,

I came to believe that the decision to place me there was based on incomplete information, and therefore was poorly made.

Fortunately for all of us, our combined voices rose up from the coiled bowels of Hell and caught the attention of a passing angel, who volleyed our anguished cries upward through the ranks until they reached the One Set of Ears That Matters Most.

Many of my fellow protestors were successful in gaining new hearings and seeing their original judgments overturned. They continue to lounge peacefully far overhead as these words are written (smiling down on me smugly, I bet). My new lot in afterlife did not include the same happy kind of promotion. Though the heat is off for now, Purgatory is my temporary home. The success or failure of this book in explaining the basics of accounting and its adaptation as the outsourced right hand of the Almighty to a broad audience of current and future judgees will tip the scales up or down.

BACK TO SCHOOL

My first encounter with AudiTrix took place soon after I died, though the fact of my death was not apparent to me immediately. Even if it had been, my faith was so long lost that the possibility of an eternal judgment coming on the heels of my demise would never have appeared on my radar. In my opinion at the time, life was mostly hard, sometimes fun, and returned us to Mother Earth, and nothing more, when it ended.

Before I knew better, it simply seemed that one morning I woke up and found myself sitting in a waiting room that looked like my dentist's. Tattered, out-of-date gossip magazines covered the cheap end tables. A fish tank in the corner sported more algae than water and hid the fish like a thick, spongy green curtain. Worried-looking people were stuffed into an uncomfortable collection of mismatched chairs. Though I had no memory of coming to be there, that fact did not bother me. Many a morning started the same way, with me going through the painful motions after a late night with no short-term memories left behind. An impaired intellect prone to spotty performance would dog me deep into the new day. That handicap made going with the flow quietly a sensible strategy.

A bored-looking receptionist slid open the glass partition in front of her desk and called out, "Luke Adams, the council will receive you now."

Feeling dazed, confused, and beset by a nasty headache, I rose and went through the same door I had seen a steady flow of people disappear beyond. Seemed strange that nobody had returned yet, I thought to myself. I looked back over my shoulder and saw that the waiting room was now empty.

The last thing I could remember was vacationing in Brazil and going hang-gliding off Rio de Janeiro's ocean cliffs. A shiver humped across my shoulder blades at the sudden vision of the craft's left wing breaking loose, sending me into a wild tailspin, corkscrewing downward into a nasty cluster of boulders in the surf. The scene went black a split second before I hit.

During this brief reverie the receptionist led the way down a short corridor and ushered me into a vast, formal-looking room, then turned on her heel and padded away on the kind of shoes hospital nurses wear. The far side was taken up by a large, raised bench that seated nine jowly men in dark robes—a stiff, somber, and purposeful group. Seated in the middle of the pack, the grayest and stiffest among them banged his gavel.

"Mr. Luke Adams, you are here to receive your final judgment."

"Is this traffic court?" I asked, recalling the crumpled mass of tickets stuffed into the largest of my desk drawers, "I really did mean to pay. Can I send in a check?"

The other eight members stared straight ahead. Only the elder acknowledged my presence, though he, too, ignored my ticket concerns.

"We have arrived at a decision," he intoned gravely, "Please review the evidence about to be presented. Should you have any objections, time will be allotted to address them."

What looked like a 1970s disco light ball descended from the ceiling and began flashing images on all four walls at once. They were images of my life, but the sequences appeared and disappeared so fast and furiously that trying to follow them only made me dizzy. I did have a vague impression that my finest hours were being glossed over, but maybe the good deeds were too paltry and few to rise above the fray.

Apparently these men of the bench had already seen the film, or were able to follow it better than I, for within seconds of its conclusion, after the regular room lights came back on but before the disco ball had been fully retracted into the ceiling, they acted decisively. Reaching into their robes in unison, each withdrew a postcard-sized piece of paper with a number written on it and thrust it high over his head, as though trying to imitate Olympic swimming judges. I had never seen negative scores in the Olympics, though. The head judge scanned the scores, glanced up at where the ball had been swallowed by the ceiling, moved his lips briefly, then lowered his head and looked me dead in the eye.

"Mr. Adams, your final score is a negative four-point-seven, and I am sure you know what that means by now. Do you have any questions on how we arrived at it?"

"How you arrived at it?" I blurted indignantly. "I don't even know what it means."

I did learn what it meant soon after. That nine-member average, no longer called the FROWN because their wisdom was coming under increasing scrutiny, had become known as the WAISTED Index, which stands for When All Is Said, Totaled, and Eternally Decided. Right or wrong or good or bad judgment mattered little because the right of appeal did not exist. It had never come up, pre-AudiTrix, back when eternal decisions were made by the One All Knowing.

"My apologies, sir, but ignorance of the law does not constitute a valid defense or point of order. Would you like a calculator to check our work? You have that right, you know."

With that, he withdrew a credit card–sized calculator from a billowing black sleeve and held it up for me to inspect.

"No, I don't want to check your work, what I want is to . . ."

"Adjourned," he called out, silencing me with a double shot of his gavel, "Bailiff, see to it that Mr. Adams gets to the elevators and is deposited at the proper ring."

A blank-faced man dressed in a white attendant's outfit emerged from a side door and took firm hold of my elbow. He was big, mean, and strong enough to be an offensive tackle for any NFL team, and his grip was not to be disputed. While my mouth flapped open and closed like a suffocating carp's, the man mountain escorted me out of the room and about twenty yards farther down the corridor. At the elevator bank he growled at a door, "Going down, ring four-point-seven."

Instantly the door opened and a final menacing look from my giant escort had me stepping lively into the car. The elevator rocketed down in a flash and the doors hissed apart, leaving me to step out alone into another room with screens on all sides. No disco ball on the ceiling this time, just four mammoth speakers mounted in the corners and bearing down like they were about to come to life, break free, and crush me.

The wall screens flashed to life in a blaze of colors and a deafening jangle of pulsating, repetitious, dentist-drill music pounded into my head from the speakers above. Suddenly I understood the full horror of it all: I was immersed in a cacophony of Justin Timberlake music videos. Since I was a lifelong music fanatic who loved all things melodic and creative, these performances were a grievous assault on everything I held dear.

Desperately I searched the room for an off switch, or at least a knob to turn the volume down. Not a single control anywhere. I flung myself into the upper corners and clawed at the speakers, trying mightily to tear them down. After that failed, I charged the walls, bouncing off them like a giant crazed moth trying to break through the glass and extinguish the light that drove it insane. None of my efforts made the slightest difference.

Falling to my knees, I raised my head and cried out, "My God, I'm in Hell!"

At once all four screens froze with the smirking face of Justin Timberlake looking at me.

"Yes, you are, you most certainly are, dude," he sang—off key.

THE INFERNO

The one piece of good news that followed the events described above is that I was not alone. For an hour every day those of us ensconced on cell ring 4.7 were allowed to leave our rooms and visit other inmates or go to the recreation center. Unlike prison, there were no worries about what we might do to each other since all of us were there for eternity and could not be killed again. Nor could anybody dole out a worse punishment than what went on in our cells twenty-three hours a day.

At the time AudiTrix seemed to take a perverse corporate glee in customizing Hell for everybody in it. This added feature was not part of its contracted mission. Whatever a person hated or was disturbed by most in life became, in dramatically concentrated form, what he or she was immersed in, like quicksand, for eternity. Though nobody on the block claimed to be a misunderstood saint, one theme emerged: the process that landed us here was a complete mystery. Were the guidelines rational? Were they arbitrary? Did the Supreme Counters make them up as they went along? Did any kind of oversight exist? Nobody knew. We worked up our courage and collectively raised our voices to the heavens in protest, and to our amazement we were heard.

We later learned that our situation was the last straw that broke the back of AudiTrix's initial operation and led to its search for a better means of judging the newly deceased. After AudiTrix had settled on earthly accounting, a member of the Supreme Council that had sentenced me brought it to the company's attention that I was in Hell largely because I had abused that very system so badly. Between that and my being the loudest and most irritating complainer on our cell ring, I was assigned the task of writing this book.

I learned about it one afternoon when the accursed show in my cell suddenly stopped and normal light filled my space. The man mountain, still dressed in his attendant's uniform, stepped in and handed me a small sheet of red paper with one sentence written in bold black type in the center. It read, "You are to take the elevator to Ring Zero and report there for your next assignment."

Looking up at my rhinoceros in white, I said, "This must be a mistake, elevators never stop at zero-numbered floors."

A voice like gravel sliding off a truck bed rose from his chest. "This one does," he said.

"But why, what is that?"

"Purgatory."

Once again he took hold of my elbow and led me to the elevator, while I again did my impression of a suffocating fish. It turned out that Purgatory was where I was to do the research and writing of this book. Not only did I have to describe accounting and its workings, I was also commanded to chronicle my greedy perversions of it. And no stone, be it inside or outside my own head, was to be left unturned. Then I had to explain how AudiTrix adapted earthly accounting to the making of eternal judgments.

By using my knowledge of accounting to steal and do a nasty assortment of other things expressly forbidden by the discipline, not to mention morality and law, I had acted as both scurrilous serpent and apple-eating sinner. A full return to the Garden was impossible after falling so far, but I was given the opportunity to slither up from Hell and into one of Heaven's lower levels if I could show why it is better to find grace in the bottom line than to steal it. If the book failed in its mission, I could be sent back for a permanent reunion tour with Justin. A new meaning had been given to "publish or perish."

Purgatory's research library has great resources, but since nobody is allowed to stay there for long, it is designed to keep inhabitants from becoming too comfortable. I spent my days, for example, in a stuffy room that appeared to have been designed for six-year-olds, complete with tiny chairs, little desks, a low drinking fountain, and an even lower toilet seat. I usually smacked my head on the way to the bathroom because the top of the door frame was level with my chin.

Here was my study, and study I did to produce these chapters in hopes of earning an upgrade to a better place, where I could at least stretch my legs without banging my shins.

Three

MANKIND'S ONE GIANT LEAP

Zero-sum games are for losers.

Merely understanding that there are benefits to working together was nowhere near enough to turn marauding bands of hunter-gatherers into building blocks of dynamic modern economies. The insight only served as an on switch for abilities humans came equipped with by nature. These had never been more than partially activated or taken too far, much like the owner of a high-performance sports car using it only to roll up and down the driveway to get the afternoon mail.

AS THE SOUFFLE RISES

What are these magic ingredients? First, humans need the capacity for rational thought so that they can act in their own best interests. This means the ability to examine a vast menu's worth of possible courses of action and pick the one that increases individual or group well-being to the maximum degree possible.

Now, any observer of human behavior, even if through a galaxy darkly from millions of light-years away, will immediately spot the problem with this. Given all of the odd and frightening things humans do, how can they possibly be considered rational? Would rational beings ever have created leisure suits, nose rings, Speedos, or Botox? Would they smoke, drink, eat deep-fried Ding Dongs, watch reality television, or become addicted to Internet sites more empty than an earthly celebrity's head?

No, of course not—genuinely rational beings would be horrified by these behaviors and never take part. But creatures with limited resources of time, talent, judgment, brains, foresight, maturity, and energy will. Humans operate within severely proscribed boundaries. Their rational horizons do not extend far, often ending before the next five minutes. This means they are only going to be as reasonable as possible, a limitation that explains a lot of things that happen on Earth, like the popularity of 1980s hair bands and lite beer.

Though keeping rationality within boundaries along even a meandering path is a tough task, keeping the instinct for fair play online and operating without crashing completely is even more difficult. This second feature leads to the creation and administration of systems of fair play where obeying the rules and doing right by others is rewarded with the same kinds of treatment; where breaking the rules, cheating, and taking advantage of your fellow beings is discouraged and punished by negative consequences.

Here again, observers of human history can quickly put together an endless list of episodes documenting mankind's terrible treatment of its own members. It is a long-running show that humans call "history." As a practical matter the bar is set well below the elimination of human brutality. It is necessary to keep the majority on the straight and narrow path most of the time, giving earthlings enough marchers to maintain their forward movement. Like bounded rationality, this target can be hit even when humanity's aims cannot be counted on to be consistently true.

OF FISH, FURS, AND FULL STOMACHS

How humans first discovered the benefits of helping each other and managed to throw nature's switch to the on position and power their great leap forward is not known. That it occurred at all, after 7 million years of spinning their wheels without gaining more than slight traction, is widely considered by observers throughout the universe to be the most unlikely success story since the Big Bang.

It probably happened by accident. Similar accidents had to be repeated many, many times before primitive humans noticed and began initiating the practice regularly. Life had been nasty, short, and brutal for a very long time. Learning to think of outsiders as beings with the potential to do good for you and yours, instead of being deadly enemies, called for a major reordering of consciousness. After pondering the achievement, a top AudiTrix executive once described it as "toilet training for the human psyche."

The following is the kind of event that may have happened: One group of hunter-gatherers has become very good at spear-fishing and regularly skewers more fish than they can possibly eat. Another group is great at making clothing from fur and has sewn together more primitive garments than they will ever need. Left alone, one group is well fed but cold, and the excess fish are left to wiggle and rot. The other group is warm and well covered but hungry, and their extra clothes are doing nothing but housing growing bug colonies.

The groups become aware of each other's situations and a collective light bulb goes off. What if excess fish are traded for excess clothes? Because of the differences in what they have and what they want, the groups value the items differently, which is the key to structuring deals that permit both sides to come out ahead while still following the rule book. The fishing clan sacrifice some of their fish for clothes and the clothing clan sacrifice some outfits for the food they hunger for. Each group comes out of the exchange better off than it entered it—a primitive version of profit.

TRUST, BUT VERIFY

Once trade had been observed to succeed on a regular basis, the practice spread and became common. The aggressive, mistrustful, violent aspects of human nature meant that trade would always rest on shaky ground, though, and it still does. Since it was saddled with so much baggage, it is easy to see why mankind's experiment with cooperation could quickly have been derailed into disaster if humans were merely rational and had no instinct for fair play. Clans would seek unfair advantages over each other through deceit, theft, violence, and intimidation—well-practiced moves from the original human playbook.

The downfall of the rationality-gone-bad approach is that a cheated trading partner will refuse to try making exchanges with the thief again. If, for example, your group traded away beautiful sets of fur-based attire and got only a few smelly, glassy-eyed, bottom-of-the-barrel fish in return, no more of those furs are going down to the water's edge.

Stir in the instinct for fair play, however, and protections take root, like customs, traditions, and laws saying that fair value received must be matched by fair value given. And when this standard is violated, a tooth is pulled for the tooth taken or an eye gouged in return for the one that was blinded. Punishments are matched to crimes.

As humans learned to cooperate, versions of the Golden Rule sprang up in all societies and religions. In each, the core value remained "Do unto others as you would have them do unto you"—a huge step forward from "Do unto others before they have a chance to do onto you." Because the Golden Rule spread around the world, it became possible not only for groups living nearby to trade with each other but also for humans to begin traveling around the world in search of good deals that could be shared. On Earth the push toward globalization was the natural result of this. In the coming years more and more planets from even the farthest reaches of the universe will be joining together in trade just as countries on Earth have.

Imagine the reactions of humans who do not like free trade on Earth when galaxization becomes the new reality!

HOLDING THE INVISIBLE HAND

Though most of the universe still regards earthlings as savages, some extraordinary people have appeared over the millennia. One man who provided the best explanation of how humans can get along by pursuing their individual self-interests was Adam Smith. He became known as an economist, but he had been a professor of moral philosophy before that. It was the perspective gained here that made his later work in economics so valuable.

Despite being human himself (AudiTrix checked because he seemed too smart for his species), Adam Smith understood human nature and its limitations. His interest was in determining which form of social organization would produce the best overall result for them.

Adam Smith looked at the progress his species had made and realized that the greatest production of wealth and progress occurred when individuals specialized in what they were best at and exchanged the fruits of their labors for other things they wanted and needed. Even though humans are self-centered by nature, they can only legally achieve the success they crave by interacting positively with other members of their species.

Suppose that a particular individual wanted only to accumulate all the wealth he could and cared nothing for other people. What is the quickest and surest route, assuming he obeys the law? Figuring out what he can use his talents to produce for which there is the highest demand and best profit potential. On his own, our friend would never rise above the level of hunter-gatherer. Simply providing enough food, shelter, and clothing for himself to live at a subsistence level would use up all his limited resources. But when he focuses his talents on making something appealing, be it a computer operating system or a better pizza, the world enriches him.

When mutually beneficial exchange occurs on a large scale, according to Adam Smith, the economy will be led to its best possible state as though guided by an invisible hand. In reality, there is no invisible hand. But there is a powerful cumulative effect from the billions of decisions made daily by individuals doing their best to improve their lot in life. Though Adam Smith emphasized the importance of free markets, where all members could spend their resources as they wished, he also stressed the importance of a strong set of laws, institutions, and traditions to discourage bad behavior and keep us playing by the rules.

The invisible hand is a critical mechanism, without doubt,

but with no invisible fence to jolt humans when they stray too far, it is useless.

WHAT WORKS FOR DAVID WORKS FOR GOLIATH

When humans began trading among themselves, simple accounting systems were developed to keep track of what they had, gave to others, and received in return. Simply cutting notches into a stick was fine when fish, fowl, furs, and figs were being collected and exchanged. But simple systems were not sufficient for long.

Within a few thousand years of learning to play nicely together, mankind began making sophisticated goods and developed currencies for buying and selling them. Now they needed a system not just for recording physical counts of particular items but for determining what it cost to make them and buy them and the resources used up to operate enterprises. Not only that, but this system had to document how good enterprises were at trading resources, with both success and failure stated in concrete terms.

The money changers had already entered the temple. The bean counters were close behind.

As the scope of businesses grew, operations could no longer be handled by Mom and Pop alone. Capital was required to grow and finance ambitious endeavors, which meant funds had to be borrowed and invested. Both lenders and owners required records of what they put into a venture, an accounting of how that venture used its resources to achieve its objectives, and an accounting of the repayments and profits to be directed back to the investors.

For this reason, accounting systems began using currencies to measure their activities. Everybody knew what money was worth. Further, only those things that could be measured in money were to be considered by accounting systems. No wild estimates or wishful thinking here. Subjectivity needed to be banished; numbers were the one thing that everyone had the same understanding of. Plenty of creative accounting went on right from the early days, of course, and many a bad number went on to do great harm, but the ideal remained. Any successful venture or economy had to aspire to it if lasting trust and consistent profit were going to develop.

Accounting's insistence on objective measurement and careful documenting of what the real costs and benefits of economic activities are has been resented by many down through the ages. Accountants are the ones who come along and tell the starry-eyed executive what his or her wonderful ideas really cost, and later write up statements showing how little revenue they generated. Accounting is the cold shower of reality that nobody likes to shiver through. On the other hand, accounting is what proves that a strategy has worked and enabled an organization to prosper. A popular movie on Earth coined the expression "Show me the money." Accounting does exactly that.

When a venture makes bad choices that cause it to decline, the accounting system records every step of the unsuccessful process, too, with objective numbers showing the money lost. This makes for a much less popular showing. There is an Audi-Trix training video on the subject, "Honey, I Shrunk the Bottom Line."

DOUBLE IDENTITY

The first book that presented accounting fit for an industrializing world was published by Luca Pacioli in Venice in 1494: *Summa de arithmetica, geometria, proportioni et proportionalita.* It was a summary of mathematical knowledge in Pacioli's day and included a description of how Venetian merchants kept accounts of their businesses. Pacioli did not invent this system of accounts, but he did codify accounting practices that had evolved into common usage. Remarkably, what he described remains the core of accounting practice to this day, on Earth and throughout the universe.

Pacioli explained double-entry bookkeeping as the core accounting mechanism. Double entries mean that every change in an account has to be offset by changes to other accounts that come to the exact same total: always, with no exceptions—ever. This means that not only are all recorded economic events required to balance, but the entire accounting system of even the largest firm, with millions of transactions being entered into it every day, has to be in perfect balance whenever all of the events are added up. Indeed, it is astounding to realize that the balance found in earthly accounting exists on a far larger scale for the entire universe.

Even in Pacioli's day the performance and pickiness of double-entry bookkeeping was regarded as boring, but what the data went on to show was not. Financial statements were generated that showed exactly what an enterprise owned, owed, and had left after all the bills were taken care of. These reflected what entities did from one period to the next by exchanging resources with the goal of maximizing wealth—and how well or poorly it went for them.

We are going to move on now and go through a series of illustrations to demonstrate how an earthly accounting system works. The operations of Hair Apparent—a business I cofounded, ran, ran into the ground, looted, destroyed, and got sent to Hell for—will serve as the platform.

Four

THE FIRST SPROUTING

Great opportunities grow from the most barren soil.

For most people accounting means dollars and cents, debits and credits, profits and losses, financial statements, annual reports, green eyeshades, and lined ledgers: in other words, a big, deadening tangle of dull, dry numbers organized in mysterious ways few of us can make any sense of. When I took accounting in college, it sure looked that way and I barely managed to pass an introductory course. What little had penetrated was lost during the happy hour that followed the posting of final grades.

Not much knowledge of any kind penetrated by the time I graduated from college, so I went back to my summer job as a carpet installer. Since high school, I had worked for a longtime installer who knew his craft inside out, from pattern to padding. At his urging I devoted myself to the business and saved enough over the next five years, with knee kickers and duck bill napping shears my constant companions, to buy a partnership stake in the business. In another five years he retired and sold his share to me. By now we had expanded into all kinds of flooring and home repair and kept a dozen crews going to handle the work.

One subject I had been interested in since childhood was chemistry. And with all the time I devoted to the business, it seemed a good place to focus that interest. Synthetic carpet is made from pellets that are melted into long strings and then twisted and shaped together to form different varieties of carpet. One Sunday afternoon while fiddling with ideas I hoped would lead to a unique kind of carpet and vast wealth, I accidentally hit on a novel process. It turned these pellets into fine strands that looked and felt just like human hair. Suddenly my new brand of rug was right there in my hands. It was useless on floors but ideal for covering bare skulls.

EARLY SHOOTS

Next I took my special fibers and dyed and mounted them on modified sections of carpet backing. Before long I learned how to make the results look just like human scalps bursting with beautiful, lustrous hair. Once these base models were produced, they could be sized and customized by heating the fibers again and styling them into shapes that remained stable yet flexible. Mounting them on human heads could be done in a flash with my own specialized carpet glue. The final result was a surprisingly realistic hairpiece that would hold up forever, even under torrential downpours, foot traffic, and tornadoes.

Despite my success in inventing such a realistic hairpiece, it did not occur to me to try making money with it. Mostly it was a hobby to have fun with. Everything changed after my first live head test. Before this I had only tried my products out on mannequins.

One night I had a woman over for dinner and, as part of the house tour, showed her my basement. That early on my processes

were far from perfected and still in the trial and lots-of-error
stage. My ten experimental models looked like they were being
eaten from their skull-tops down by acidic blobs of rhubarb jam
slathered on with a trowel. My goal had been to refine the glu-
ing process. Her goal was to get up the stairs and out the door
before I could turn her into subject number 11.

Mr. Allan Borland, a local builder who used my company for
all his carpeting, was my first live head case. It began when I
visited him at the site of a new home one morning to go through
the measuring and settle on the right style, brand, and price. He
had arrived early and was leaning against the front of his truck
when I pulled up in mine. It was a windy day and it amazed me
to see how long the strands were that he normally kept combed
over his bald head. Seized by the passing gusts, they looked like
skinny blades of beach grass in a hurricane.

Glumly he looked my way, "Yeah, I know, I look ridiculous
with my hair blowing all over the place. I should have worn a
hat, but I forgot."

"No, Mr. Borland, it doesn't look . . ."

He cut me off with an impatient wave of his hand, "Luke, it
looks awful. It's time for me to just accept the little hair I have
left for what it is and cut back the comb-over."

A thought popped into my head. "Have you ever tried a hairpiece?"

"You mean a toupee?" he responded, "God no, I've never
seen one that didn't look awful."

"What if I could show you one that looked so real you
couldn't tell the difference, that could be any color and style you
want and never wear out or look bad?"

Borland eyed me suspiciously.

"Son, you do carpet and floors. What could you know about
hair?"

"How about I show you?"

Being careful not to get entangled in his weblike strands as they blew in the wind, I used my tape measure to record the area and slope of Borland's head.

"For God's sake, hurry up, Luke," he pleaded. "If anybody sees you measuring my head, they'll think my brains have flown out of it."

Two days later I stopped by his house with the new hair packed in a lady's hat box. He tried it on without the glue, sure that he would not want it resting on him for more than a few seconds. While he examined his new reflection in the hallway mirror, a scream erupted from the top of the stairs. We both jumped and turned to see his wife standing there, covering her mouth and pointing at Borland.

"Oh my goodness, Al, I thought I'd walked thirty years back in time . . . your hair . . . how did you get it back?"

All he could do to explain was point at me.

Once Mrs. Borland understood the nature of the hair and how it had come to its perch on her husband, she insisted I glue it in place. I did as she instructed and waited until it dried to make sure we had a tight, shiftless seal. When I left, the happy couple was seated on their living room love seat. She was running her hands through his new mane while he cooed like a pigeon in love.

Late that night Borland called to say that he and a fellow bald friend, who was so impressed with Al's new look that he insisted on one of his own, wanted to go into business with me. The three of us would form a partnership that sold hairpieces unlike anything the world had ever seen on a cranium.

"By the time we're through," Borland exclaimed, "bald spots will be on the endangered species list!"

A STAR IS BORN

I agreed to the partnership on the condition that I got to keep the hair process to myself as a trade secret. This also meant that I would produce all the hairpieces on my own, apart from our new venture, and sell them to the business at cost. All profits and losses would then be divided equally among the three partners. In addition, I would receive a salary for daily management of the operation and would hire others to run my carpet and flooring business. My partners would keep their businesses, which were much bigger than mine, and function as silent partners. Overall decision-making power would be shared equally.

We named the business Hair Apparent.

Daily management included performing the accounting functions. It was not a task I felt comfortable taking on, but with limited funds available we decided to wait until the business showed some healthy growth before we hired a real accountant.

Though accounting seemed confusing and fussy back in college, I was surprised at how straightforward and logical it proved to be in practice. That it was necessary to run and make a living from Hair Apparent provided a wonderful incentive. Not only did the accounting tasks make sense, once I mastered the basics the whole system became simple and routine to run. It made so much sense and became so easy, in fact, that it did not take me long before I began thinking up ways to abuse my own system.

Five

FROM FOLLICLE TO FOREST

Dullness is the best repellent.

To show how accounting systems work, we will examine a simplified version of Hair Apparent in the next few chapters. As you will learn, these systems are based on a few simple principles that are not difficult to apply. They are so easy to work with, in fact, that I was able to go from setting up an honest business to committing fraud on a massive scale in just a few short weeks.

Among my scandals and crimes, I almost managed (but not on purpose) to turn our customers into victims of chemical beheadings with a potion any witch doctor would envy. While this and many other disasters were in the works, I covered my tracks with a set of books so bland nobody who bothered to look would find them worth taking a second glance at.

We will get to all the gory details and provide the first honest accounting of them later. Before those can be understood, however, it is necessary to have a solid foundation in accounting. So let us begin with a look at the transactions that occurred at the launch of Hair Apparent.

IN THE BEGINNING

We three partners breathed life into Hair Apparent with an initial investment of $90,000 each. For the other two it amounted to a side bet, but for me this was a huge sum of money—my life savings, in fact. But I felt confident about our prospects. Hair Apparent would be offering the first environmentally friendly hairpieces: sustainable hair for those cursed with deforested heads.

First, we found a storefront building, complete with working cash registers, in a good location that was the right size for us. We paid $100,000 for it. Our next purchase was two thousand hairpieces for $10 each from my separate manufacturing operation, Hair Today (we will look at its accounting system a little later). These base model hairpieces would be dyed, styled, and shaped to customer specifications in our store. After an extensive search I found a machine, originally designed to make artificial turf, that could be modified to do all of that. Even better, the tasks were easy enough that anybody could be trained to operate the equipment. Including alterations, it cost $95,000,

Next, came the purchase of $4,000 worth of supplies, bought on credit. With this, we had invested in most of the things we would need to get the business started.

RULES TO COUNT BY

No matter how large, small, complex, or simple a business, accounting systems organize all accounts into three categories: assets, liabilities, and equity. The three are defined below, and all of Hair Apparent's transactions will fit into one or another of these categories.

WHAT IS OWNED, WHAT IS OWED, AND THE LEFTOVERS

Assets are things a business owns or has a claim to.
Liabilities are the debts it owes that must be repaid.
Equity is the owner's stake in the business—what
   remains after the liabilities have been settled.

The things we spent money on initially were assets, and the money itself was an asset. A new firm's goal is to invest in assets that it then uses up in the course of doing business and exchanges for other assets. For example, we purchased the assets necessary to offer hairpieces for sale in hopes of exchanging them for money from customers. If we were successful at it, the money flowing in from customers would exceed the money we paid to have our products flowing out.

No matter how well or poorly our business did at covering those broad, open spaces our customers came to us so distressed about, its accounting system would always balance, just like every journal entry has to (see Pacioli on double-entry bookkeeping). This accounting equation can be stated in two different ways:

IT ALL COMES OUT A WASH

$$Assets - Liabilities = Equity$$
or
$$Liabilities + Equity = Assets$$

Always being in balance does not mean there is no change, however. The exchanges that a business engages in cause it to grow and prosper or shrink and decline. And just because everything balances does not guarantee all is well; a firm can go down blazing like the *Hindenburg* and its accounting system will remain in balance until the last ember flickers out.

Transactions are recorded with journal entries and each entry causes the accounting equation to change. Every entry consists of at least one credit and one debit. The number of debits and credits do not have to match, but their totals must. Debits and credits have a simple job to do: they record the increases and decreases in the accounts that result from doing business. The table below shows how debits and credits are used to make asset, liability, and equity accounts go up or down. If this does not make perfect sense right now, don't worry: you will soon get some examples of debits and credits in action.

Ups and Downs All Around

	DEBIT	CREDIT
Asset	Increase	Decrease
Liability	Decrease	Increase
Equity	Decrease	Increase

In the old days all economic events were first recorded in the general journal by hand. It served as an initial staging area. From there, data would be separated out and organized and then sent on its way to become information that was useful in analysis and decision making. Today, the process is the same, except the entries are tapped into computers rather than scrawled on pages. For purposes of illustration we will stick with how they look in traditional form.

As you can see from the example below, debts are offset on

the left and credits on the right. This is always so and applies to the account titles and the dollar amounts. It also makes it possible for debits and credits to be added up in separate columns. Thus, it is easy to make sure the totals agree, as Pacoli decreed long ago.

This is the basic balancing act that journal entries follow:

Debits $$$$
        Credits $$$$

Prior to the arrival of computers, when accounting was done by hand, there were bookkeepers who did little else day after day but write entries in the general journals. It was a vital function but one of the dullest jobs ever invented, though it did have the advantage of being very safe, since few people were willing to fight for the right to do it. One of AudiTrix's early creations of an individual Hell, in fact, was to make somebody who hated accounting do journal entries with a dull pencil for eternity.

It was not a completely original idea. The myth of Sisyphus inspired it, and the goal was to create a fate worse than pushing a rock up a hill for all eternity, only to see it roll back down after a final grunt and shove had gotten it to the crest. Every time it looked like the long list of journal entries was finished, and just a second after the debit and credit columns balanced following a series of torturous errors that had to be fixed, the entire general journal would be wiped clean, as though a fiendish strain of disappearing lead were at work. Then the process would start all over again from scratch. The wailings from this pocket of Hell were particularly agonized.

Now we can apply what we learned above and use debits and credits to record the early sproutings of Hair Apparent. This includes the initial investment by the owners and the assets we purchased to prepare the business for opening. In Table 5.1 explanations are provided below each journal entry to help them make sense.

Marking the Trail

TABLE 5.1 GENERAL JOURNAL ENTRIES

	DEBIT	CREDIT
Cash	270,000	
Owner's Investment		270,000

The three owners of Hair Apparent each invest $90,000 in the business. This increases the asset cash and the equity account, owner's investment, by the same amount.

	DEBIT	CREDIT
Building	100,000	
Cash		100,000

A building is purchased. Because it is paid for with cash (in the form of a check, which is treated the same as cash), the asset cash goes down. Another asset, in the form of the building, goes up to reflect the purchase. We estimated that the building would last twenty years.

	DEBIT	CREDIT
Inventory	20,000	
Cash		20,000

Two thousand base model hairpieces are purchased for $10 each. Cash goes down by the purchase amount. The asset inventory goes up as a result of the purchase.

| Equipment | 95,000 | |
| Cash | | 95,000 |

Equipment was purchased, which caused the corresponding asset account to rise. Cash, used to pay for it, went down. We estimated that the equipment would last for five years.

| Supplies | 4,000 | |
| Accounts Payable | | 4,000 |

Because supplies were bought on credit, a liability to establish the debt arises. Supplies, an asset account, also rises.

| Total | $489,000 | $489,000 |

As the total shows, debits and credits add up to the same amount, as Pacoli decreed must always be so.

The general journal is a straightforward document, as we have just seen. The next step for the data recorded is, too. After the journal entries for a particular day or period are entered, they are posted to ledger accounts. Ledger accounts are simply places where transactions of the same kind are grouped together. Cash, for example, gets its own account. This makes it much easier to keep track of where it came from and where it goes to than if the entire general journal had to be scoured. It also keeps clear exactly how much cash has come in or gone out—or should have.

When postings are made, reference numbers are used so that the original transactions can be traced back to their origin. Say you are looking at the cash ledger and see an amount that looks suspicious. You can follow it back to the original entry and find a brief description of the particular economic event, along with information on the parties involved if you want to follow up some more. Doing this creates trails forward and backward and provides an excellent mechanism for guaranteeing not just that the mechanics of the system are working properly but that the humans involved are being competent and honest. In short, it is a good firewall against breakdowns and thievery. A crucial point to keep in mind is that the firewall has not been built that human ingenuity cannot scale or tunnel underneath.

The ledger accounts will be shown after we have more economic events to add to them. Right now we will jump to the next step, producing a balance sheet that displays the status of all our accounts on a specific date.

FREEZE FRAME

A **balance sheet** provides an overall financial picture of
   a firm by listing its assets, liabilities, and equity on a
   specific date.

A balance sheet groups assets together first, then liabilities, then equity. Just before Hair Apparent opened its doors to the pillaged pates of the world, our balance sheet looked like this.

A Picture Before the Prom

Hair Apparent Balance Sheet January 1, 20__

ASSETS

Cash	$ 55,000
Inventory	20,000

Supplies	4,000
Building	100,000
Equipment	95,000
Total Assets	$274,000

LIABILITIES & EQUITY	
Accounts Payable	$4,000
Owner's Capital	270,000
Total Liabilities & Equity	$274,000

TALE OF THE TEA LEAVES

Without ledger accounts to show how the ending account balances were determined, we will look at the transactions themselves. The most active account was cash. It came to life with the $270,000 invested by the partners and was reduced by $100,000 spent on the building, $95,000 for equipment, $20,000 for inventory, and $4,000 for supplies, leaving us with $55,000. The remaining asset accounts stayed at the amounts spent to buy them. Moving on to liabilities, we see the $4,000 account payable for supplies purchased on account and the owner's investment of $270,000.

FROM HAIR TO THERE EVENTUALLY

So far this is accounting at its most basic. All we tracked was money invested in a new business and the first few assets bought with it. This particular balance sheet, then, is simply a portrait of an enterprise in waiting—for its doors to open and customers to come through. What happens then is much more important. Once a firm begins engaging in trade with customers, events are occurring that provide evidence not just of how sound their judgment was in deciding on a particular product to sell or industry to do business in but of how good a job they do at turning these assets into more assets and setting the stage to be even more successful in the future.

Six

FROM PELLET TO PERFECTION

No magic compares to the talent for growing a seed into a star.

By inventing a new and vastly improved kind of hairpiece and offering it to consumers suffering from ravaged foliage on their upper decks, Hair Apparent was out to succeed as an entrepreneurial enterprise. Simply opening up a business does make an individual or firm entrepreneurial. Real entrepreneurs get to know their target markets inside and out. They develop innovative goods and services designed to meet an unfulfilled, or not yet realized, desire and present their products to the market in the most appealing way they can think of.

Contrary to popular belief, entrepreneurs are not just brazen operators out on the cliff's edge eager to risk everything on a leap into the dark. True entrepreneurs try to cut the risks of their undertakings to the point where they become the most attractive option available. This takes a lot of work and a healthy dose of intuition. My success with turning carpet pellets into hairpieces was a rare case, for it really was a shot in the dark that hit a target I had no clue was out there.

Entrepreneurship is a rough-and-tumble process because the

new and different offered by the entrepreneur attracts con-
sumer dollars that used to be spent on the old and now in the
way. A brilliant Austrian economist, Joseph Schumpeter, used
the term "creative destruction" to describe the process whereby
economic growth and wealth are sparked by entrepreneurs
who redirect consumers' spending of their limited resources to
more attractive choices. Those on the creative end of the process are richly rewarded when they succeed and do wonder-
fully well. Those on the destruction end experience mounting
losses and the end of their businesses, unless they change in a
hurry.

THERE'S A NEW KID IN TOWN

At Hair Apparent we were the upstarts out to take business
away from the established hairpiece manufacturers. We did it
by giving customers a product that was cheaper, looked better,
and lasted longer. If our business was successful, the accounting system would document our superior skills by booking
steadily increasing sales, new asset acquisitions, rising net worth,
and nice big bottom-lines that kept getting bigger. For those
competitors unable to keep up, their fake hair would gather
dust while ours flew off the shelf. Their accounting systems
would record mounting losses, bad debts, declining equity, and
bottom lines plummeting deeper and deeper into negative ter-
ritory.

One thing we knew for sure: few people believe bald is beautiful, and an aging population means millions of bare spots
yearning to be covered. We did not expect the world to beat a
path to our door just because we had built a better mousetrap,
but we did know plenty of customers were out there. The Ro-

man poet Ovid wrote in *The Art of Love,* "Ugly are homeless bulls, a field without grass is an eyesore. So is a tree without leaves, so is a head without hair." Nothing about this opinion had changed by the ninth century, when Scheherazade asks, "Is there anything more ugly in the world than a man beardless and bald as an artichoke?" And nothing had changed by the time we reached out to modern-day "artichokes."

Accounting is the language of commerce. Without entrepreneurs there would be little for accountants to write about in their journals. Without accounting, of course, entrepreneurs would lack the ability to accurately measure their success. In short, accounting uses numbers to chronicle the adventures of entrepreneurs.

Now it is time to look at the adventure that commenced when Hair Apparent opened its doors for business.

DO NOT MIX WHAT MUST BE MATCHED

In the last chapter we left off with Hair Apparent's balance sheet after we invested money into the business and then spent most of it on assets necessary for our start-up operations. Now we will look at the first month's sales of hairpieces and record the results with journal entries. From there we will show how ledger accounts work and draw from them to produce an income statement.

Every sale of a hairpiece meant money had come in for a product that went out the door tightly glued to a customer's head. As owners, our equity went down by the cost of the hairpiece and up by the money received. When these exchanges took place, they were recorded with expenses and revenues along with changes in assets. This gave us a record of what had to be sacrificed in order to bring in more resources.

In Chapter 5 the only financial statement we looked at was the balance sheet. This is because no exchanges with paying customers had taken place yet. Now it is time to examine what goes into an income statement. An income statement begins with the top line, which is the sales revenue. From there it deducts different categories of resources that were sacrificed to generate the top line and ends with the bottom line, or net income. If net income is positive, then more resources, as measured in cash, came in than went out. If net income is negative, fewer resources came in than went out, resulting in a loss—which shrinks the firm.

FLOWS AND EBBS

An **income statement** is a record of the resources flowing into a firm (revenues) during an accounting period and the resources sacrificed (expenses) in order to generate them.

For Richer or Poorer

During an accounting period, revenues and expenses are recorded with debits and credits. The same rules apply to these as to equity. This is because revenue and expense accounts used during an accounting period have their balances transferred to an equity account (retained earnings) at the end of the period to show how much owner wealth grew or how much it shrank. Here's how debits and credits are used to record revenues and expenses.

	REVENUE	EXPENSE
Debit	Decrease	Increase
Credit	Increase	Decrease

Out of the Gate

During our first month of business, Hair Apparent recorded several economic events, listed in Table 6.1. Most will appear on the income statement. After this list come the journal entries. Explanations are included for all of them, so if anything is confusing below it should be cleared up quickly.

TABLE 6.1 ECONOMIC EVENTS, JANUARY 20—

A. Sold 900 hairpieces for cash, at $25 each
B. Sold 1,000 hairpieces on credit, at $25 each
C. Paid $12,000 for radio and television advertising to air throughout the month
D. Collected $19,000 of accounts receivable
E. Bought 2,500 hairpieces with cash for $10 each
F. Paid off $2,900 of accounts payable
G. Sold 2,400 hairpieces on credit at $40 each
H. Building depreciation: $417
I. Equipment depreciation: $1,583
J. Used up $1,900 of supplies
K. Bought $2,300 of supplies with cash
L. Paid salaries of $20,000 to employees
M. Paid a contractor $8,400 to repair the building
N. Owed income tax expense of $4,100; not been paid

O. Paid $1,200 for utilities at the end of the accounting period
P. Revenue account closed into retained earnings
Q. Expense account closed into retained earnings

A Record of the First Running

As economic events and exchanges happened, our accounting system recorded them in the general journal. Traditional journal entries come with brief explanations, but in Table 6.2 we have expanded on them a bit to keep things clear and explain a couple of items, like depreciation and closing entries.

TABLE 6.2 GENERAL JOURNAL ENTRIES

	DEBITS	CREDITS
A. Cash	22,500	
Cost of Goods Sold	9,000	
Inventory		9,000
Sales Revenue		22,500

The asset cash increases by the $22,500 charged for the hairpieces. Inventory, another asset, goes down by the $9,000 Hair Apparent paid for the products that are no longer in their possession. Both of those assets are shown on the balance sheet. The numbers are used twice so that an income statement can be produced. The $9,000 cost of goods sold is an expense (outflow of resources) and the $22,500 is revenue (inflow of resources).

B. Accounts
Receivable   25,000
    Cost of Goods
Sold   10,000
        Inventory   10,000
        Sales Revenue   25,000

The difference between A and B is that in B sales are made on credit, with accounts receivable the asset account recording what will be collected in the future. The rest of the entry is put together as A was.

C. Advertising
Expense   12,000
        Cash   12,000

Cash has been spent on advertising, causing the asset cash to be reduced and expenses to rise.

D. Cash   19,000
        Accounts
        Receivable   19,000

Cash was increased because some of the customers who made purchases on credit paid for them. This means that the receivables asset must go down by the amount no longer owed.

E. Inventory   25,000
        Cash   25,000

Hair Apparent purchased more hairpieces and put them in inventory, an asset account. Paying for them means that the asset cash is reduced.

F. Accounts		
Payable	2,900	
Cash		2,900

By paying a debt Hair Apparent causes accounts payable, a liability account, to go down. Because cash was used, it too goes down.

G. Accounts		
Receivable	96,000	
Cost of Goods		
Sold	24,000	
Inventory		24,000
Sales Revenue		96,000

Just as in B, above, Hair Apparent made sales on credit.

H. Depreciation		
Expense,		
Building	417	
Accumulated		
Depreciation		417

Depreciation expense is an estimate of the portion of an assets value that has been used up in an accounting period. The credit to accumulated depreciation is used to reduce the value of the asset by the same amount. We arrived at the depreciation expense by dividing the building's cost by its estimated useful life (100,000/240 months = 417)

I. Depreciation
   Expense,
   Equipment   1,583
                 Accumulated
                 Depreciation   1,583

As in H, above, the cost of the asset was divided by its estimated useful life to get the depreciation expense (95,000/60 months = 1,583)

J. Supplies
   Expense   1,900
                 Supplies   1,900

The expense here reflects the amount of supplies used up during the month. This also causes the supply asset account to go down.

K. Supplies   2,300
                 Cash   2,300

Supplies were replenished. The supply asset account goes up by the purchase, and the asset cash goes down by the amount spent.

L. Salaries
   Expense   20,000
                 Cash   20,000

The salary expense shows what we paid our employees. This caused cash to be reduced.

M. Repair
    Expense   8,400
          Cash   8,400

Money had to be spent making normal repairs to the building, like fixing stairways and leaky plumbing.

N. Income Tax
    Expense   4,100
          Income Taxes
          Payable   4,100

The tax expense shows what we owed the government for the month based on Hair Apparent's income. It increased the liability income taxes payable because the money had not been paid yet. In fact, I do not think it ever was, which was one of the things that helped land me in Hell.

O. Utilities
    Expense   1,200
          Cash   1,200

The utility expense represents things like electricity, natural gas, phone service, and water used during the month.

P. Revenues   143,500
          Retained
          Earnings   143,500

Here we have a closing entry. Revenue and expense accounts are used as temporary places to accumulate the revenues and expenses of a specific period, in this case a month. Because revenues are shown as credits, a debit equal to the total revenues of the period brings the balance to zero, and a credit transfers it to an equity account, retained earnings. The increase here shows how the inflow of resources caused the value of the ownership interest to go up.

Q. Retained
   Earnings   92,600
            Expenses   92,600

This closing entry is for expenses. As in P, above, for revenues, this brings the balance in the expense account to zero and transfers it to retained earnings and the equity account. The amount tells us how much the resources sacrificed during the period caused the value of the ownership interest to go down.

Some simplifying was done in order to make the recording above go smoothly. The 5,700 hairpieces sold happened throughout the month, for example, but for our purposes it made sense to combine them into two journal entries. Overall, what you see above is pretty much how things occurred during the first month. I had to figure out how to set up and work our accounting system on the fly, but it did not turn out to be nearly as complicated as I expected.

A few things did throw me. For example, recording a revenue amount twice, as we saw in A, B, and G did not make sense at first. But when I realized this made it possible to have two separate financial statements showing different aspects of our operation, things fell into place. We need the balance sheet to tell us what assets, liabilities, and equity are on a particular date. We need the income statement to show us the resources that flowed into our firm during an accounting period, as revenues measured in dollars, and the resources that were sacrificed in order to generate revenues, as expenses measured in dollars.

The income statement's bottom line, the net income or net loss for the period, gives us a final count of how much better or worse off we are as a result of the decisions made about how to exchange our limited resources during the accounting period. It is also what links the income statement and balance sheet because the net income or loss is seen also in a firm's equity rising or falling.

We will see how all of this works in the financial statements, but first it is helpful to look at the ledger accounts journal entries are posted to. If all of this sounds tedious and dull, it is because the mechanics of accounting systems are tedious and dull. This is a good thing. Think of your accounting system as being like a furnace on a cold day. Nobody wants anything exciting going on with the furnace. You want it to work reliably, just as it always has, a simple, predictable, dull process. But if it breaks down, a crisis is not far behind. Nobody goes into the basement to watch the furnace operate because it is so exciting; similarly, accounting procedures are not exciting to witness. The difference between the two is that if your furnace breaks down, you can call in a service to have it fixed. But if your accounting system breaks down, not only are you held responsible for it, but you better know what has to be done to repair it. Otherwise you will end up in your own private Hell, like me.

One of the things that put me on that express elevator to the inferno was violating a basic accounting concept, the matching principle. Because accounting systems record economic activity, it is very important to know how much we had to sacrifice in expenses (outflows of resources) for revenues (inflows of resources) generated. This is the only way to know how well or how poorly a business has performed.

THROUGH A GLASS CLEARLY

The **matching principle** means:
- Revenues are shown with the expenses that were incurred to generate them
- Revenues and expenses are recorded in the periods they occur

Amassing the Troops

Following the ledger accounts in Table 6.3, we will see the matching principle in action on the Hair Apparent income statement (Table 6.4). Remember, all that is happening with the ledger accounts is that increases and decreases in the same accounts are being grouped together. As you will quickly notice, this provides information that is a lot easier to analyze than if you had to search through endless journal entries.

The numbers in the ledger accounts without letters next to them are from the first set of transactions where we spent money on assets. The rest use the same letters as the original journal entries, making it easy to trace them back and forth. Just as in the journal entries, numbers on the left side are debits and those on the right are credits.

TABLE 6.3 HAIR APPARENT LEDGER ACCOUNTS

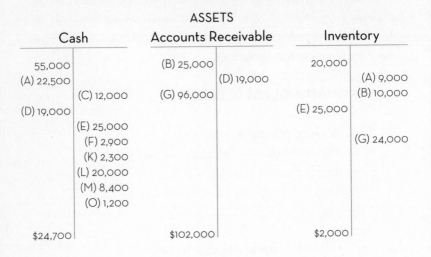

ASSETS

Cash		Accounts Receivable		Inventory	
55,000		(B) 25,000		20,000	
(A) 22,500			(D) 19,000		(A) 9,000
	(C) 12,000	(G) 96,000			(B) 10,000
(D) 19,000				(E) 25,000	
	(E) 25,000				
	(F) 2,900				(G) 24,000
	(K) 2,300				
	(L) 20,000				
	(M) 8,400				
	(O) 1,200				
$24,700		$102,000		$2,000	

Supplies		Building		Accumulated Depreciation	
4,000		100,000		(H) 417	
	(J) 1,900				
(K) 2,300					
$4,400		$100,000		$417	

Equipment				Accumulated Depreciation	
95,000					(I) 1,583
$95,000					$1,583

LIABILITIES

Accounts Payable	Income Taxes Payable
	4,000	(N) 4,100
(F)2,900		
	$1,100	$4,100

EQUITY

Owner's Capital	Retained Earnings
270,000			(O)143,500
		(O) 92,600	
$270,000		$50,900	

Revenues	Expenses
	(A) 22,500	(A) 9,000	
	(B) 25,000	(B) 10,000	
	(G) 96,000	(C) 12,000	
(O) 143,500		(G) 24,000	
		(H) 417	
		(I) 1,583	
		(J) 1,900	
		(L) 20,000	
		(M) 8,400	
		(N) 4,100	
		(O) 1,200	
			(O)92,600
-O-		-O-	

FIRST TASTE OF SUCCESS

TABLE 6.4 HAIR APPARENT INCOME STATEMENT, JANUARY 31

Revenue		$ 143,500
Cost of Goods Sold		43,000
Gross Profit		$ 100,500
Other Expenses:		
Salaries	$20,000	
Depreciation	2,000	
Advertising	12,000	
Repairs	8,400	
Supplies	1,900	
Utilities	1,200	
Income Taxes	4,100	
Total Other Expenses		49,600
Net Income		$49,900

TALES FROM THE TEA LEAVES

At the beginning of our first month, the accounting equation balanced at $274,000 worth of assets and $274,000 of liabilities and equity, as seen in our balance sheet from Chapter 5. At the end of the month, however, our accounting equation tipped the scales at $326,100 of assets and $326,100 of liabilities and equity. Where did the increase come from? You can see it clearly laid out in the income statement. We sacrificed $43,000 of hairpieces as expenses (cost of goods sold) in exchange for $143,500 of revenues from customers, who left our establishment with happier heads than they entered with.

Cost of goods sold does not account for all the resources we used up during the first month. In order to operate the store, we had to pay salaries; use up supplies; pay for repairs; consume power, water, and phone service; and show the taxes due on our earnings. In addition, because there was wear and tear to the building and equipment, depreciation expenses were taken to show the portion of these assets values that were used up to do business. Total resources valued at $92,600 flowed out of Hair Apparent, and in return, $143,500 of resources flowed in. This left us better off in the amount of $49,900.

By putting that $49,900 of net income into retained earnings, we show how much the ownership interest increased as a result of a profitable first month of doing business. Our financial statements tell us more than this, too, and we will examine the information gained from them in Chapter 7.

On a final note, our profit was a pretty healthy percent of revenues, especially for a new business in its first month. Bear in mind that it is not just the materials and labor that went into the hairpieces customers were paying for or the expenses to operate the store. They were also paying for our expertise: the ability to produce a desirable product at an attractive price.

Seven

HAIR ON FIRE

Good financial statements are mirrors. Bad financial statements are funhouse mirrors.

W hat in the world is that noise?" Al Borland, my noisy silent partner, asked. He'd come striding through the store entrance the second I unlocked the doors for a new day of doing business with the bald. Our theme song stopped him in his tracks.

"It's 'Magic Carpet Ride,' a huge hit back in the 1960s. We play it at the top of every hour the store is open," I answered.

A blank look came across Al's face.

"I don't get it."

"Our hairpieces are made of synthetic carpet pellets but look better than any of the brands made from normal materials. It's magic, right?"

"If you say so," he replied, his right hand unconsciously rising to gently weave its way through his hairpiece. "They look so real I forget what they're made of. Customers aren't offended by the song?"

"Nobody has complained yet, and we've got more business coming in than we can handle."

Al shrugged. "Far be it from me to argue with success. And success, by the way, is what I came to talk to you about. I thought that if we just broke even for the first month we'd be doing fine, but we made a decent amount of money right out of the gate, and it looks like things are only going to get better from here."

We were three days into our second month and I agreed with Al's assessment. I'd sent him the first month's financials the night before, and in reviewing our sales growth, I saw that after a slow couple of weeks in the beginning, things had taken off and it appeared that we were riding a powerful upward trend.

I looked around at the various hairpiece models on display. Inspired by my song choice I had used mannequins to display our wares and tried to shape their faces to look like a variety of rock stars. Even though I had some famous names represented, from Paul McCartney to Bruce Springsteen, nobody had figured any of them out yet. A much bigger concern was that the increase in business had put a serious strain on my hairpiece-making capacity. Stocking up for the store's opening had been easy, but replenishing inventory and keeping up with increasing demand were challenges I did not know if I could handle. Already my inventory was dangerously low.

"I assumed it would take longer for us to catch on, too, but business is great. The thing is, I don't think I can keep up on the manufacturing end."

Al clapped his hands together and gave me an approving nod.

"That's a perfect lead into what I wanted to talk about. Look, Luke, I've been in business a long time and done pretty well, but this right here is a unique opportunity. We've got something special cooking. What I'm thinking is that we should bring in some more investors and really get this thing going big time, then start opening up more stores, and maybe franchise the operation."

"A franchise?" The idea startled me. "A franchise for hair-piece stores. What would we do, offer drive-through toupees, maybe sell sideburns as side dishes?"

My partner chuckled at that. "Maybe that's not a bad idea, but look, if you can make those things here, why can't we set up manufacturing sites in other places?"

I paused a moment to mull that over.

"I guess we could. Hey, we could advertise ourselves as the only providers of freshly prepared hair."

"There you go. I like how you're thinking," Al replied. His enthusiasm propelled him right past the fact that I had been kid-ding. "As for your being so busy, how about we raise the money and let you expand your operation with it? I know, I know, you want to keep your process a secret, so we, as the business here, can invest in whatever it takes to support your other operation and let you run with it. We'll keep the same deal, too. Just make the hairpieces and sell them at cost. Hell," and here he paused to wink conspiratorially, "maybe even put in a little markup for yourself."

An idea about that markup flashed through my head. Al would not have liked it.

"How about I put some feelers out and see who ponies up to the table?"

"Well, it can't hurt to ask," I responded, "and I could sure use some more resources on the manufacturing end."

Al slapped me on the shoulder. "Onward and upward, then," he said, and turned to march back out the door. A few steps before it he turned around. "Hey, I wanted to tell you, not only are people complimenting me on the new hair, they say my face looks younger, too. And you know what? When I look in the mirror, I see what they mean—it's almost like I had a mini face-lift or something."

I took a close look at his face.

"You know, now that I look, I agree, you do look more youthful. Did the fountain of youth bubble up into that hot tub of yours?"

Al waved off the question and laughed. "Aw, I know I don't look any different—it's just the hair talking. Okay then, I'll be in touch." With that, he left the building.

Al really did look younger and it worried me. A couple of weeks earlier I had noticed a strange phenomenon with some of the hairpieces I had tested my glue on. Over time it caused the carpet backing, which the artificial hair was mounted on, to shrink. My assumption had been that this was due to the glue drying out, something not likely to happen on top of a warm, moist head. But maybe it was happening with Al. This alone would not have been a big concern. I could simply remove the hairpiece and find a different kind of glue to put it back in place. And this is where the other glue issue came into play: as it shrank, it fused with whatever it was attached to.

LET THE NUMBERS DO THE TALKING

Within an hour of leaving the store, Al called my cell. He sounded excited and out of breath.

"Okay, we're on for eight o'clock this evening, my place. You can make it?"

"Make what?" I asked. Business had picked up fast and between the morning rush and wrestling with the issue of the shrinking hairpieces, I had completely forgotten our earlier conversation.

"The meeting with investors, remember?"

"Geez, Al, we talked about putting one together, but I had no idea you meant so soon."

"Gotta strike while the iron is hot, or the fish biting, or whatever," he exclaimed, "You can make it?"

I thought it over for a moment.

"Well?"

"How about this: we make it two nights from now, same bat time, same bat place, and I'll put together a presentation they can look at."

"Hmmm, I hate to put it off, but having something to show them, besides my beautiful new head of hair, makes sense. Good thinking. Let's do it."

"You need to check with them first?"

"It's done."

We would meet in what All called his rec room. I called it the bat cave. When Al built his new house, he designed the basement with a much higher ceiling than normal. The space was enormous. When you entered, it did look like a rec room—for a sheik. This section of the vast cavern was equipped with two pool tables, a Ping-Pong table, three foosball tables, a home theater complete with popcorn machine and mini stadium seating, and enough exercise equipment to train a football team.

Things got serious in the other part of the basement. There was a meeting room big enough to seat twenty people comfortably. It was outfitted with a computer projector, a sound system, and all the office equipment you could ask for. Adjoining it was Al's office. The desk had the surface area of a small battleship and was usually covered with models of upcoming building projects.

The plan was to serve dessert, coffee, and cocktails, let everybody get comfortable, and then knock them out with my presentation. That investors would be interested in launching a chain of artificial-hair stores that would spring up wherever hair fell down might sound strange, but our history, as brief as it was, gave reason for faith in a profitable future. We had a product nobody else knew how to make (a trade secret I closely guarded), it was cheaper than all of the alternatives, and it looked much better and lasted lots longer. We had the Mercedes of hairpieces and it came with a Yugo price tag.

Eight

INTO THE SHARK TANK

Set your hook before the fish turns fowl.

Mere visions of wealth are not enough to convince sensible investors to open their wallets. They need solid numbers that provide objective measurements and realistic projections. How did Hair Apparent meet this standard after so little time in existence? It was not my presentation's leadoff slide, a saying I had created to break the ice, "Build a better hairpiece and the bald will beat a path to your store." But their heads snapped to attention a few slides later.

I had graphed how gross profit per unit shot up when the unit sales price increased. We began the month by charging $25 for hairpieces that cost us $10 to buy and then only another $3 for cranial customization, allowing us a gross profit of $12 per hairpiece. This translates into 48 percent per unit, a healthy gross profit margin.

We had set the initial sales price at $25 because I wanted it to be far enough below the established competition that the low price would grab attention immediately and lure customers into our store. The strategy worked, of course, but further investigation showed that we were so far below what competitors charged that we had room to work with. When I raised the price to $40 later in the month, nobody complained and the pace of sales actually picked up. Now we were at a 68 percent per unit gross profit, and it became obvious that this, too, could be improved on in the future. I did more research on competing products and concluded that our hairpieces easily matched up with those selling in the $300 range. Since I was continuing to work on improvements, new models could be expected to keep getting better.

Near the end of my presentation I passed around samples of competitors' products for our potential investors to compare with my own. A few men self-consciously put the competing products on their heads and examined the differences with hand mirrors I had placed in the middle of the conference table. Mine clearly was the best fit, head after head, and when I described plans for future models that would take us to the next level, all eyes lit up. The only misstep of the night came when I unveiled the prototype of my pride and joy, the combination Donald Trump/flock of seagulls (a 1980s hair band) creation I called the "Billionaire's Beak." Everybody except me agreed that it would never fly.

The investors also liked our strong cash position and the fact that accounts receivable were already flowing in steadily. The store was proving to be easy to staff and run, with low expenses and ongoing maintenance. Most attractive of all to them, however, was an asset that did not show up in either Hair Apparent's or Hair Today's balance sheets. It was far more valuable than everything else: my trade secret.

Back when I first saw that my process for making humanlike hair from carpet pellets worked, I considered patenting it. That would have given me sole rights to produce the stuff for twenty years, but my patent application would have to explain the process for making it. The application would become public knowledge, meaning that anybody could order a copy and see how I did it. Copying my process exactly would be illegal, but nothing could prevent an innovative person from looking at what I had accomplished and figuring out how to do something similar without violating patent law. As Colonel Sanders had done with his eleven herbs and spices many years earlier, I opted to keep my creation a trade secret.

The wonderful feature of trade secrets is that there is no time limit on them. Nobody can produce the item so long as the owner of the secret goes to reasonable lengths to keep it secret. Because my hairpieces were the result of a few simple procedures that no rational person would ever think of, I decided to leave no paper trail anywhere, not under lock and key or even in a safe-deposit box. I preserved it within a much harder shell: my own skull.

Because earthly accounting devotes itself to using only numbers that are objective, verifiable, and without doubt, it only shows the costs of developing trade secrets or buying them from another entity. There is no estimate made of what they may ultimately prove to be worth. In the eyes of the potential investors we were pitching to, this meant that on paper our enterprise's true value was vastly underestimated. Investing in us would be like buying into a gold mine for the price of a parking lot.

By the end of the evening the atmosphere in the room was like a shark tank, full of restless beasts impatiently circling and more than ready to feed. To my surprise, Al, who had the reputation for being able to corral even the sharpest toothed predators, sounded a note of caution.

"Now boys, let's not go overboard here. This is a new thing we got going after all—it's only a month old."

"Now, Al," the most corpulent and fully haired among them said, "could it be that you really want to keep this to yourself—maybe just want us as small supporting players to add some cash while you keep control, not to mention most of the bucks?"

Al lowered his head and shook it sadly.

"Harold, how long have we known each other, huh? And you think I'd do something like that?"

Harold slapped his big, meaty hand on the table with a mighty guffaw. "It's because I've known you so long that my antennas went up!"

"You sure you're not just excited about the chance to add even more money to your fortune?" chimed in the youngest among them, who looked relieved when the others laughed.

"You guys," Al responded, like a good-natured patriarch who couldn't say no to friends, "you're all worked up, which is good, believe me. But keep in mind we're only just into our second month."

"It's not the length of time," chimed in another of the jolly men. "It's the forward motion and where it appears to be taking you."

"Uh, yeah, I think we all agree, if I understand what Junior over there just said," the elder among them chimed in, a man in more need of our product than Al had been.

"You've got a gimmick or gizmo that beats the pants, er . . . I guess hair, off the competition, hands down. After looking over the information you e-mailed out this afternoon, I did some homework. You didn't think I'd just roll over and take your word for it, did you?" He asked me with a wicked grin, and then stepped over to give Al a playful punch on the shoulder. The same hand then dipped into his jacket pocket and came out with an entirely different proposal.

"This is a great investment opportunity, and we aren't disputing that a bit. But how about we buy the operation and do our own thing with it? The three existing partners can walk away with millions in profit after being in business only a few weeks. I think you'll be pleased at what we are offering. Take your time to look it over. We'll wait."

AN EMBARRASSMENT OF RICHES

It turned out to be some pretty impressive homework. They wanted to buy the business and my patent and keep me around for two years to solidify what had so recently been started. Here's a summary of their offer:

Keys to the Kingdom

FIRST HAIR APPARENT OFFER

Equity of Hair Apparent	$ 320,900
Synthetic hair trade secret	5,500,000
Two years exclusive services of Luke Adams	2,350,000
Hair Apparent name	1,400,000
Total	$ 9,570,900

As you can see, the quantifiable number in the offer is the smallest amount. A firm's equity, we have learned, is what remains after total liabilities are subtracted from total assets. It is also referred to as a firm's net worth. This number is arrived at by following the rules and should come out to be the same, or close, no matter how many different accountants calculate it. Everything else in the offer is speculative.

Being offered $5,500,000 for the trade secret stunned me for two reasons. First, the process was so simple, and stumbling across it had been pure luck (I was not paying close enough attention to the experiment and allowed the temperature the pellets were processed at to climb dangerously high, which led to the hairlike result). Second, the large number meant they were very optimistic that there would be a strong market for the product for many years to come. With all the risks and uncertainty that come with doing business of any kind, they were willing to pay a huge amount for a product that had barely been launched in only one geographic area. These guys were smart investors, so they had to be expecting future profits that were worth many times what was being offered.

What they wanted to pay me to stay involved was equally surprising. They could not know, of course, that what I did was so simple. Convinced that my presence was critical to the ongoing operation, it made sense for them to offer enough to gain my full commitment. For all they knew, I could have a slew of brilliant ideas I was chomping at the bit to launch. The truth was, this one happy accident was it—nothing else was bubbling away on a back burner anywhere.

Al scanned the offer quickly and asked his guests, "You mind if my partner and I talk this over in my office? It won't take long and there is plenty to eat and drink here."

Indeed, there was a huge spread laid out on a side table that nobody had touched yet. Al grabbed my sleeve and pulled me into his office.

The instant the door shut behind me I blurted out, "Al, this is unbelievable. We're got to take their offer. I never dreamed we'd make this kind of money."

"Calm down and let's think it over," he said, a lot less excited than I was. "These guys are no dummies. If this is what they're offering, you can bet your bottom dollar it's worth a lot more. And based on what you laid out tonight, our future looks even better than they were assuming when they put this offer together. I say we stick with letting them invest a limited amount and see where this ride takes us."

Stunned, I asked him, "Are you nuts?"

"Not a bit. We'd be nuts to settle for an offer that's probably tens of millions less than we'll end up making."

"But there's no way to know that, Al. I say let's grab the offer while the grabbing's good. You know, taking the bird in hand instead of waiting for the two in the bush?"

"What are you talking about?"

"I don't know. I thought the saying would make sense to you. Anyway, our partnership agreement says all three partners have to agree on any offers, so if you say no go, then no go, and I don't know what Frank thinks. But I really . . ."

"Good, then let's go tell them that. By the way, Frank's committed himself to voting however I say, which is why he isn't here," Al said, and was out of his chair and through the door before I could say anything else.

Our investors were not surprised when Al turned them down. I was still hoping for a mind-changing miracle to come upon him and didn't speak. A minute later I was incapable of speaking at the shock of their next offer. They had commandeered the computer projector and flashed it on the broad white wall at the head of the room:

Keys to the Kingdom and Beyond

SECOND HAIR APPARENT OFFER

Equity of Hair Apparent	$ 320,900
Synthetic hair trade secret	8,500,000
Two years exclusive services of Luke Adams	4,350,000
Hair Apparent name	2,000,000
Total	$ 15,170,900

Though struck mute by the size of the new offer, I was fully capable of jumping for joy and was starting to do just that when Al opened his mouth and ruined everything.

"You guys are too much," he told them, as though they had pulled off a good-natured prank, "Won't give up, huh? Well, me, Luke, and Frank are sticking to our guns, right, Luke?"

All I could do was stare back.

"Let's stick with the original plan and put together some dollar amounts you can invest. If you're still interested, that is."

Al flashed us his best grin. I wondered if his teeth were any more real than his new hair.

"Gentlemen, start your checkbooks!"

Nine

THE PERILS OF PROFIT

All trust and no suspicion equals insanity.

With the future profitability of Hair Apparent and their own visions of riches dependent on my continuing to be cooperative about the use of my trade secret, the existing partners and our new investors alike allowed me almost unlimited freedom. I was the goose laying the golden eggs and could "nest" however I wanted to, with few questions asked or limitations forced on me. They reasoned that because I profited from hairpiece sales just as they did, there were good incentives to run the accounting system and my separate company, Hair Today, honestly.

They were wrong on both counts. Before long goose eggs were all they had to show for their faith in me.

Passing on that astounding offer ate at me in ways nothing ever had before. Vast wealth and a life of plenty had been dangled in front of my face and then cruelly snatched away. Al and my other partner, Frank, were already wealthy. How could they deny me the same opportunity, especially when our success was all me? For the sake of my sanity and fair play, I told myself, it was justifiable to start being a little creative about finding ways to get my innovation and hard work to begin paying off in the present instead of waiting until I was their age.

Once it dawned on me that dipping my beak into our streams of cash and other resources could be done without interruption, I began stealing with the gusto of a rookie running back smashing his way through a hole in the defensive line that opened up on every play. I started big and bold, by telling them that new machinery was urgently needed to increase the production of hairpieces to newly anticipated levels that far exceeded our original estimate.

Not true.

The conversion process that transformed synthetic carpet pellets into long, silky strands of fake hair was surprisingly fast and efficient. My current equipment, which was still new and much better than what I invented the process with, was more than equal to the task. Where I had trouble keeping up came in the hands-on labor, the job of feeding those synthetic pellets into one end of the machine and cutting the long strands of hairs that emerged at the other end into sections. These sections had to be bundled and formed into rough shapes while they were still warm, fresh, and moist and then mounted on squares of modified carpet backing.

I told our new investors that $2 million of the newly infused cash was needed for the immediate purchase and installation of new equipment for Hair Today. They balked at first but started to come around after I provided them with a breakdown of how much additional product could be produced, and money made, once it was up and running. Because my process for making the hairpieces remained off-limits, my partners and investors had no idea how easy it was to make our products.

They assumed it must be a high-tech marvel and regarded

me as a slightly paranoid creative genius who was irreplaceable. I did nothing to correct them. What they should have done was insist the process be evaluated by an independent group of outside experts, but I certainly was not going to mention it. They would have found out that it was about as complicated as making cotton candy.

"You've got to spend money to make money, am I right?" I asked them on a conference call.

"Yeah, sure, but it's our money you're spending," came the reply from one of the more stubborn investors.

Feeling cocky, I leaned back in my chair and replied, "It is, and if you want I'll be happy to return it to you and bring in some of the other interested parties who want to get involved in this situation."

Harsh whispering followed my answer. It sounded like all of them were in the same room and sharing the same speakerphone.

"Luke?" came a new, much more ingratiating voice, "How about you provide us with some information on this equipment so we know what we're talking about here? I'm sure it won't be a problem. After all, anybody who gets out of the gate like you did must have a powerful sense of direction for the finish line."

"I'll e-mail you everything there is to know about it first thing tomorrow morning, how's that?"

"That's great," the voice of investor reason told me, "and since we don't want to slow things down, we'll get back to you within a day."

"That's great," I told them.

And it was great. With just the software I possessed, it was an easy matter to take the pictures and specs from the equipment I already had and inflate them into a larger, very convincing-looking model, complete with mind-numbing detail on its workings and an exhaustive owner's manual and service plan. It probably caused the eyes of any investor who actually looked through everything to glaze over immediately. They signed off on the purchase two hours after I sent the information.

Though the $5 million injected into Hair Apparent was a huge jump in cash-on-hand and in the potential scope of our operations, nobody noticed that the scope of our accounting system needed to expand also. I remained the only one overseeing the accounting function, and nothing I did had to be checked by anybody else. Not only was the fox in the henhouse—the fox had just been given millions more birds and a giant fryer.

My first major act after the new money flowed in was to open a few secret accounts with different banks in Liechtenstein. Feeling tricky, I also set up two shell companies so that the money would go from Hair Apparent to them first, then to Liechtenstein. Unsure of how far I would be able to take things and if the day would come when I had to make a quick exit, I organized everything on my home computer so that the transfers could be made in seconds when the time came. A small fortune would be waiting for me in any one of a number of select locations well before I got there.

My first purchase, or so I dreamed, would be of a seventy-five-foot houseboat equipped with every luxury, a floating McMansion.

A SWEATSHOP IN EVERY CELLAR

The truth was that I only needed another two sets of hands and they were already working for me. Three years earlier, after my carpet-installing business became busier than ever, I hired a woman to clean my house and do some shopping, meal preparation, and laundry. Her husband usually picked Esther up after she finished, and over the course of a few conversations I learned that he had been a highly skilled carpenter in their native country, the Dominican Republic. Not long before I hired Esther, they had come to the United States on temporary visas to work at a new resort in the Catskills. The resort closed and they headed up north to live with his brother while they decided what to do next. They were in the process of applying for American citizenship but were not confident about their chances.

A few weeks prior to the grand opening of Hair Apparent I asked Esther, "Hey, how would you like to pick up some more hours?"

She was in the middle of making a week's worth of dinners that would go into the freezer for me to thaw out as I wanted them. Her cooking was great, so the meals never lasted more than a few days.

"Am I not doing everything you have hired me for?" she asked, sounding concerned.

"Esther, you are wonderful at everything I hired you for, especially the cooking," I replied, as I reached forward and grabbed a not-yet-wrapped-up meatball and popped it in my mouth, "The idea is to see if you want to try something new and earn some more money."

Her eyes narrowed.

"It does not mean going into the basement, I hope?"

Esther found my lowest level creepy and went down there only when absolutely necessary. Given the disturbing variety of mutant-rock-star-looking mannequins sporting different types and styles of hairpieces on their heads, in every shape, size, and color imaginable, I could not blame her. And then there were the piles of finished hairpieces waiting to be loaded onto my truck and brought in to replenish Hair Apparent's inventory. They made my basement look like the lair of a serial scalper.

"We can fix it up some, if that's what you mean."

With a meaningful look she told me, "Some things cannot be fixed, Mr. Adams."

"Okay, here's what we'll do then. If the mannequins creep you out, I'll enclose the lab where I work on new products and keep the manufacturing separate. What I need you to do is just be there a few hours a day to feed pellets into the machine and section off the product that comes out and glue it to the backing strips. It's easy and I'll pay you a little more than your normal rate for it."

"And I will not have to see any of those ugly dolls?"

"Never, I swear it."

"I do not know, Mr. Adams. It is a tempting offer, but being down there all alone frightens me."

"All right, how about if I give you a raise for everything you do, not just the new job in the basement?"

"How much will it be?"

I told her.

She took a step over to me, smiled, and shook my hand.

"We have a deal, then, Mr. Adams."

"And you're sure the mannequins being in the next room won't be a problem?"

She waved me off dismissively. "Who could be silly enough to fear dolls with bad hairdos?"

During that first month business grew quicker than expected, and Javier, Esther's husband, began working with her regularly. Given his skills, this proved to be a great addition. He maintained the equipment better than I did and fast began coming up with ways to improve the production process.

A few days before I fled the country I came home to find Javier waiting for me at the front door. Smiling proudly, he held out what looked like a mink stole.

"Feel this, Mr. Adams, it is so soft."

I ran a pair of fingers over its surface and nodded in agreement, "Yes, it is—have you been hunting out in the backyard?"

"No, no, sir, I have been hunting on the machine, for a way to make fur from your pellets."

"You mean this isn't real?"

"It is no more real than your hair, Mr. Adams, I mean the hair you make, not the hair on your head," he added quickly.

"Amazing. You know, you might have something here."

"Yes, yes, I know. Yesterday I watched a show on television about people protesting; they said it was wrong to wear fur and were very upset at those who do."

"Lots of animal activists get upset at the business, no question about that."

"So what if, like with your hairpieces, we make furs that look and feel better even than the real thing, and that cost so much less they cannot be resisted?"

Javier had gotten hold of something great. I encouraged him to keep working on it and said he was free to use whatever was available in my basement workshop in his spare time. Events of the next few days interrupted my ongoing interest in the project, but Javier had all the encouragement he needed and kept at it vigorously.

COSTS WITHOUT CONSCIENCE

Even before pirating the money earmarked for new hairpiece-making equipment, I had already begun to line my pockets by fudging the numbers. Prior to launching operations, I gave Al the $10-a-hairpiece price I would charge our store. The cost was accurate then, but at the time I had no incentive to make them cheaper. We had not yet opened for business, so no exchanges had been made between the two operations. Once I started making that first batch to transfer from my basement to the store shelves, however, I quickly developed ways to make profits that would never be documented.

When one is producing goods, there are three categories cost accounting systems track: direct materials, direct labor, and manufacturing overhead. Direct materials become part of the goods being produced. For the hairpieces this included the pellets, chemicals, carpet backing, and adhesive. At the outset of operations this cost was $2 per hairpiece. Direct labor is the hands-on work going into making a product. Based on my ability to make fifteen hairpieces per hour and an hourly rate of $75, this cost was $5 per unit. Overhead includes manufacturing costs necessary to make an item that do not become part of it and include a variety of costs, such as depreciation, rent, and utilities. Going by what I paid for my living space, use of equipment, and the costs to power everything, overhead came to $3 each.

When all the manufacturing costs were added, the estimated unit cost to me was $10. I originally agreed to sell to Hair Apparent at the same cost because I, along with my two partners, would benefit when they were sold at a profit. The accounting I did for the unit costs was honest and accurate—at first. Because we made money right out of the gate, nobody questioned my manufacturing methods or checked up on my processes or cost estimates. It occurred to me that a little number fudging could go a long way toward bringing in extra revenue as the business grew. A lot of number fudging would increase my personal wealth that much faster.

I started with labor costs for Esther and Javier, paying each $15 an hour and not withholding taxes. At this rate (with no taxes or benefits to worry about), I could hire five workers for what I paid myself, and labor cost per unit dropped to $1.

The next step was to search out a cheaper supplier of synthetic carpet pellets. Because my new hires worked more carefully and efficiently, they could make what I had with fewer materials. Materials per unit now dropped to $1 per unit, just as labor had.

Overhead costs per unit fell, naturally. With more workers producing more units, without having to pay for additional equipment or space, the overhead cost per unit dropped to $2. What about the $2 million of equipment on the Hair Apparent books? Even though it did not exist, I intended to depreciate it over the next four years. This meant claiming a $500,000 expense every year. The business would not get the entire amount as a benefit, but it would reduce our taxable income by a lot. So if our federal and state tax rate came to 40 percent, for example, we stood to save $200,000 in taxes ($500,000 × 0.40 = $200,000).

As the company's only golden-egg-laying goose, I convinced myself that continuing to charge $10 per hairpiece even though the actual cost per hairpiece had dropped to $4 was perfectly okay. Without my secret recipe nothing at all would be cooking, but with it bubbling away all partners and investors could feed at the table. Before long I convinced myself that they did not deserve the feast that was coming, so why not put them on a diet? They would never know.

There was no reason to stop at pocketing an unreported profit of $6 per hairpiece. Within days of ratcheting up production I made up a story that costs were rising in sync with more units being produced. Not just for labor and materials but for overhead, too. More space was needed, utilities would go up, and the costs of operating the new equipment were also higher. In truth, the huge basement offered more than enough space for Esther and Javier, and my power bill did little more than inch upward as output increased.

My associates were not pleased by the news that manufacturing costs per hairpiece had jumped to $14. Though they balked, none among them knew accounting. When I provided them a detailed (and thoroughly false) explanation of our product's cost structure, they lost interest quickly and agreed to the new unit price before they came close to getting a handle on it. Now, instead of selling the hairpieces to Hair Apparent for $10 each as previously, I made a profit of $10 on each one ($14 price – $4 cost).

Covering my scheme was easier than covering the heads of our customers because I did the books for both businesses. For example, when Hair Apparent bought the next three thousand hairpieces from my manufacturing operation, I recorded it as follows:

	DEBIT	CREDIT
Inventory	42,000	
Cash		42,000

As for the Hair Today records, I used the same doctored cost I had convinced my partners to accept. My basement couple were not on a government-approved payroll, so I continued using the labor rate I earned back when I was still making the hairpieces. In doing so I hid the profit made and avoided paying income taxes on it. A fraud in one place was reflected and offset by a fraud in another: I recorded the sale like this for Hair Today:

	DEBIT	CREDIT
Cash	42,000	
Cost of Goods Sold	42,000	
Inventory		42,000
Revenue		42,000

My plans quickly evolved into a scheme for franchising Hair Apparent in the years to come. As part of the deal, franchise owners would have to buy their hairpieces from the sole authorized provider, Hair Today. And why not bring investors into Hair Today right away? With an agreement like that, the millions of dollars coming my way would dwarf what I had just raised for Hair Apparent.

It would just take a few well-placed basement shops to make all the hairpieces needed to cover every inch of bald flesh the world over. Then I would have billions.

Ten

FOR WHOM THE TOUPEE TOLLS

The only things rarer than perfect numbers are perfect men.

t was thirty minutes before opening and I gazed out the front window and considered my next moves. By now a bunch of customers had come in all excited about their suddenly youthful faces. Just the day before, I had received my first panicked call from a man whose face had begun tightening too much. He compared the feeling to a winch on his sailboat being turned a time or two beyond the optimum.

"I know it's crazy to think a hairpiece could pull my skin back, but I swear, Mr. Adams, it feels like the thing has a grip on the top of my head and is bearing down and tightening it. And I know this sounds crazy, too, but the hairpiece is getting smaller, almost like it's crumpling up into a ball while it pulls my skin into itself."

"We have received some reports of shrinkage," I told him, and forced myself to deliver the lie in a calm, soothing voice. "It seems that a small number of customers are allergic to the materials, and the resulting reaction makes it feel like the hairpiece is getting smaller and. . . ."

"No, no, you don't understand. This isn't shrinkage, like with a new pair of pants in the dryer. This is a major constriction, like. . . . like . . . like if the whole continental United States was being inhaled by Delaware."

"Customers in the past have reported the very same feeling, sir, and in every case the hairpiece soon relaxed and went back to its regular shape. Once that happens we will be happy to remove it and refund your money."

"How long did it take before the hairpieces loosened up?"

"How long have you noticed the problems with yours?"

"Hmmm, about four or five days now."

"In all cases so far, relaxation occurred on the seventh day, at which time I personally removed the hairpieces. In all but one case, the customers chose to have new items installed, free of charge, of course, rather than take a refund."

"Why can't I have the thing taken off now? It's like having a living creature trying to eat through my skull, for God's sake."

Adding a touch of scientific authority to my voice, I replied, "I wish that were possible, sir, but when the adhesive is in a contractionary state it fuses with the base surface and the only way to remove it is to harvest the surface also."

"What does that mean? Please be straight with me."

"Unfortunately, sir, it means skin removal would be a necessary part of the process."

Quickly I pulled the phone away from my ear to avoid going deaf from the shout that followed, "You mean to tell me my only hope is to be scalped?"

"Oh no, nothing like that, I assure you. Once the piece loosens to its former tension, we can remove it easily. In fact, let's schedule a time for you to come in, first thing in the morning, two days from now, and I will attend to it personally. This is a rare side effect and we are very sorry. I assure you, we will make it right."

"I hope so. I don't want to get my lawyer involved and all

that, but this has got me spooked and it needs to be taken care of."

"I understand fully, sir, and give you my word that you will be well taken care of."

I had bought myself a little time there, but before I could relax too much it looked like my time was at hand. Al Borland's S-class Mercedes screeched to a halt outside. He burst out of the car like a Tasmanian devil and made a beeline to my door. He looked worse than I could have imagined. The hairpiece had contracted into the shape of a large doorknob on top of his head. It looked like the kind of tight hair knot worn by sumo wrestlers during competitions, except the skin around it was completely bare, not even a wisp of fake or real hair broke the drum-tight smooth surface.

Al came blasting through the front door and planted his squat frame in front of me. With his face raised up, his nose was just a couple of inches from my chin. I took a step back. Al advanced a step.

"Oh no you don't, buddy boy," he said, wagging a thick index finger at me, his voice a wet, lisping rasp. "You're going to stay right here until I get some answers, *capisce?*"

A wash of spittle sprayed across the lower half of my face with the last word.

"Sure, Al, sure, I'll do whatever I can. My God, what happened to you?"

I knew perfectly well what had happened to him, but I did my best to sound shocked and surprised. The shocked part came naturally, what with his facial skin pulled up so far that his upper gums showed when his lips parted.

Al stabbed at the knot on top of his head like he was getting ready to spear it with his finger.

"See this? See this monstrosity on top of my head?"

"Of course I do, Al, but I don't understand why you changed the hairpiece so much—it looked great on you the way it was."

He roared as powerfully as possible out of a mouth stretched too tight to open and close properly, "I didn't do anything to this succubus on my head. I swear to God, it started shrinking at first, and then the thing began pulling my skin into itself. It's like this hell-beast came to life and started to inhale my skin, you understand?"

"Uh, well . . . uh, why don't we . . . uh . . . ," I stammered.

"Why don't we what, boy genius? I can't get the damn thing off my head. I tried yanking it off, but it's on so tight my head would come off my shoulders first. Then I tried cutting it off with scissors—nada. Then I tried a belt sander and a power saw. Nada again—it was like trying to kill The Blob, for Christ's sake."

Suddenly Al surged forward and clutched the front of my shirt tight in his fists, "What should I do, Luke, what should I do? You've got to help me before this hair ball from hell eats me up completely. You've got to help," he repeated, his fevered eyes boring into mine. The skin on his face was drawn so tight the effect was like an overinflated balloon one last breath away from exploding.

"I do think I have a solution, Al, but you're going to have to let go of me so I can show you, okay?"

"All right, but no monkey business, you got that?"

"Sure, Al."

The instant Al released his hold on my shirt, I bolted for the storeroom in back and headed out the door leading into an alley. It connected to a network of other alleys and streets, and I charged into them. I heard him cutting loose with a stream of obscenities interlaced with my name as I rounded the corner.

Eleven

WHEN A PICTURE FAKES A STORY

Numbers will confess to what our consciences never admit.

Al was not the kind to grin and bear it when calamity struck or tried to bore its way into his skull. Though the locked-in-place grin made him look maniacally happy, his psyche was stretched tighter than the skin over his cheekbones and he would come after me relentlessly. Fortunately, I had a plan in place for when disaster struck and this certainly qualified as a worst-case scenario come true. Now that the dark secret of my adhesive had been revealed, it was time to work those Liechtenstein accounts.

Before we go into the details of my unsuccessful flight from massive fraud—which ended very badly—we should see a clear statement of what I had done to deserve the fate that soon caught up with me. So let us take a look.

Even though I had already brought in somebody to do most of the day-to-day accounting, I remained the only person authorized to make more than small cash transactions. I had sole access to the password that enabled transactions to be done online. After it was long gone, the cash on Hair Apparent's books would appear the same because I made no recording of

my thefts. Checks would begin bouncing soon, though, because I left only enough in there to cover a few small bills. At
this point, in fact, nothing would look out of the ordinary, even
though the reality was every bit as alarming as Al's disappearing face.

FROM HAIR TO THERE EVENTUALLY

To illustrate the progression from promising new business to
fraud-infested disaster, three balance sheets, some journal entries, and two ledger accounts are shown below. The first balance sheet gives us Hair Apparent's status at the beginning of its
second month, which also reflects where we left off with our
ledger accounts in an earlier chapter. The second balance sheet
is a status update that includes the $5 million in fresh investor
money and also reflects the phony $2 million investment in new
equipment.

From there the situation goes ugly. My fraudulent activities start crawling into the light with journal entries that show
their impact on the firm's resources, along with a pair of ledger accounts that track the damage done to our cash account
and net worth. The third balance sheet of shame reveals the
terrible reality that emerges after all the lies have been erased
and the true numbers enter into the accounting. Not a pretty
sight.

To begin with, let us start with what seemed to be a hopeful
picture, a view of what our assets, liabilities, and equity looked
like on day 1 of month 2.

Days Before the Storm

HAIR APPARENT BALANCE SHEET
FEBRUARY 1, 20___

Cash	$ 24,700
Accounts Receivable	102,000
Inventory	2,000
Supplies	4,400
Building	100,000
Accumulated Depreciation, Building	(417)
Equipment	95,000
Accumulated Depreciation, Equipment	(1,583)
Total Assets	$ 326,100
Accounts Payable	$ 1,100
Income Taxes Payable	4,100
Total Liabilities	$ 5,200
Owner's Capital	$270,000
Retained Earnings	50,900
Total Equity	$ 320,900
Total Liabilities & Equity	$ 326,100

The balance sheet presents a rare thing: a business entering its second month, already profitable and poised to do even greater things in the future. With a healthy income in month 1, a unique product nobody could duplicate, and a huge untapped market eager to hide the light reflecting off their bare heads with bushels of fresh, fake hair, only good things appeared to be on our horizon.

Our new investors agreed with this point of view and put up $5 million, all the while arguing with great enthusiasm that we should take more of their money. It took some convincing, but they went with my suggestion of Hair Apparent buying equipment for my separate business, Hair Today. Though the investment was made in good faith and the purchase of new equipment for Hair Today was not, both looked legitimate when they were recorded.

Documenting Deceit

	DEBITS	CREDITS
Cash	5,000,000	
Owner's Capital		5,000,000

To record the investment of $5,000,000 in Hair Apparent.

	DEBITS	CREDITS
Equipment	2,000,000	
Cash		2,000,000

Equipment is purchased for cash.

The new investors bearing gifts of cash knew the money went where it was supposed to go—at first—because their checks were cashed by Hair Apparent quickly. None of the new investors or existing partners, however, checked to see if the money flowing from their pockets into Hair Apparent's accomplished the stated purposes. Their lack of curiosity meant that nobody would discover that I had created fake companies—but with real bank accounts—and transferred money to them. And if the phony equipment purchase was beyond anyone's power of detection, who among them would detect that the path had already been cleared for huge sums to leave the country?

Absent the knowledge of the flight of a big chunk of our new money, the picture presented in the second balance sheet shows a business with great prospects made even more promising with a huge addition of funds. Anybody looking at our cash position and upcoming opportunities in general would likely be chomping at the bit to throw their own money into the pot, too. A look at the swelling balance sheet makes the reasons clear.

Bulked Up and Ready to Roll

HAIR APPARENT MID-MONTH BALANCE SHEET

Cash	$3,024,700
Accounts Receivable	102,000
Inventory	2,000
Supplies	4,400
Building	100,000
Accumulated Depreciation, Building	(417)
Equipment	2,095,000
Accumulated Depreciation, Equipment	(1,583)
Total Assets	$ 5,326,100
Accounts Payable	$ 1,100
Income Taxes Payable	4,100
Total Liabilities	$ 5,200
Owner's Capital	$5,270,000
Retained Earnings	50,900
Total Equity	$5,320,900
Total Liabilities & Equity	$ 5,326,100

What lurked behind the numbers soon emerged and acted like a wrench thrown into a churning engine. It brought everything to a screaming halt. The ugly truth was that no equipment had been purchased with that $2 million of investor money. I also leveraged our impressive cash balance to borrow another $3 million from a local bank as long-term debt. Nowhere did I record this transaction—except as an entry in my personal, and very private, set of financial information.

From here the thefts cost less but were equally abusive of the trust placed in me as the one responsible for the functioning of the accounting system. I used the company credit card to buy $6,500 in airline tickets and prepaid hotel rooms. With supplies on hand that were necessary to the operations of Hair Today, I could not resist the temptation to take some of them. I carted off $3,300 worth. And while I was at it, why not create paychecks for nonexistent new employees and direct-deposit the earnings into another set of bank accounts that could easily be rolled into my own? This quickly yielded another $22,000. It also occurred to me that as accounts receivable were collected, which all came from prior sales of our wares on credit, it would be easy to take this money, too. I was right, to the tune of $101,000.

A Traitor's Tale

For this last set of thievery I did not even try to cover my tracks with false accounting entries; I simply did not record anything. Because my plan was to leave the country with as much cash as I could squeeze from the business, I did not want to do anything to call attention to it. The results, though, were devastating to Hair Apparent. In the table that follows are journal entries that serve to accurately update the accounting system and document, at least partially, the financial damage done by my thievery.

TABLE 11.1 THEFTS AND LOSSES

	DEBITS	CREDITS
A. Cash	2,000,000	
Equipment		2,000,000

Cash never spent is added back to the cash account and equipment never purchased is taken off the books.

| B. Loss on Theft | 2,000,000 | |
| Cash | | 2,000,000 |

Cash falsely stated to have been spent on equipment is shown to actually be a loss to theft.

| C. Cash | 3,000,000 | |
| Long-Term Debt | | 3,000,000 |

Previously unrecorded bank loan is added to the accounting records.

| D. Loss on Theft Expense | 6,000,000 | |
| Cash | | 6,000,000 |

To record money taken from Hair Apparent and not documented: $3,000,000 raised with long-term debt and $3,000,000 of investor funds.

| E. Loss on Theft Expense | 22,000 | |
| Cash | | 22,000 |

Money paid out to nonexistent employees is shown as a loss.

F. Loss on
   Receivables
   Expense   101,000
                  Accounts
                  Receivable   101,000

Receivables collected and taken from firm are accounted for as a loss.

G. Loss on
   Supplies
   Expense   3,300
                  Supplies   3,300

Supplies taken out of the firm without the removal being journalized are documented

H. Loss on Theft   6,500
                  Accounts
                  Payable   6,500

Liability for flights and hotels unrelated to firm travel is established.

I. Retained
   Earnings   8,131,800
                  Expenses   8,131,800

Theft losses are closed out of the expense account and transferred to retained earnings.

Early Evidence

We need not go through all the affected accounts in detail, but it is worth examining a few of them more thoroughly to see the scope of what I pulled off. Below are ledger accounts showing what happened to cash and expenses and the impact on retained earnings when expenses were closed into that account.

CASH		
Beginning Balance	3,024,700	
	(A) 2,000,000	
		(B) 2,000,000
	(C) 3,000,000	
		(D) 6,000,000
		(E) 22,000
Ending Balance	2,700	

EXPENSES		
	(B) 2,000,000	
	(D) 6,000,000	
	(E) 22,000	
	(F) 101,000	
	(G) 3,300	
	(H) 6,500	
		(I) 8,132,800
Ending Balance	-O-	

RETAINED EARNINGS		
Beginning Balance		50,900
	(I) 8,132,800	
Ending Balance	8,081,900	

As the above ledger accounts make clear, my actions not only drained Hair Apparent of cash but brought us to the point where we were left with negative equity. Every loss written off as an expense reduced the value of the owner's interest. Nobody but me (and I was busy robbing the company blind) paid any attention to how money was being used until most of it, and all of me, was already gone. By the time my partners and the investors were forced to finally examine the books (with plenty of help), Hair Apparent had been looted and left so badly devastated that bankruptcy became a foregone conclusion.

The Ugly Truth

The balance sheet below presents the true picture of the shape I left Hair Apparent in, and it is shocking—especially when you consider how healthy our business and its future outlook had been just a few days earlier.

HAIR APPARENT BALANCE SHEET
MID-FEBRUARY 20—

Cash	$ 2,700
Accounts Receivable	1,000
Inventory	2,000
Supplies	1,100
Building	100,000
Accumulated Depreciation, Building	(417)
Equipment	95,000
Accumulated Depreciation, Equipment	(1,583)
Total Assets	$ 199,800
Accounts Payable	$ 7,600
Income Taxes Payable	4,100

Long-Term Debt	3,000,000
Total Liabilities	$ 3,011,700
Owner's Capital	$ 5,270,000
Retained Earnings	($ 8,081,900)
Total Equity	($ 2,811,900)
Total Liabilities & Equity	$ 199,800

Despite my taking enough money to leave Hair Apparent destitute, it was not the asset loss that did the most harm. The worst damage came from the loss of things that did not appear directly on the financial statements. What could they be? For one thing, the value of my trade secret and the expertise that came with it. Without my process for producing low-cost, high-quality hairpieces, and the documented prospects for generating new and improved products and broadening our market reach, Hair Apparent had no future. The very things that made the firm so promising turned out to be the seeds of its destruction: because I was such a key player, nobody dared question me, and I used my position to steal without limit.

BRANDING THE FUTURE

Another huge asset loss not reflected in journal entries or the financial statements was Hair Apparent's reputation. Even if I had never stolen from the company and chose instead to stay and try to repair the damage, it probably was too late. Once it became common knowledge that my hairpieces had gobbled up scalps like a starving wolf, who would take a chance on one? No amount of reassurances or promises can repair a reputation whose value has turned so steeply negative as to bring business to a halt.

Twelve

VACATION PLANS

You can run and you can hide, but you cannot escape yourself.

Being out of Al's sight and shouting range was of no comfort. I feared that his hideously smiling, homicidal face would pop up at any time and charge me, like a target on a police firing range turning the tables and stalking the shooter. Or maybe he would be planted in my path, waiting there when I rounded a corner, with a real grin in place of the fake one because he had outsmarted me so easily.

An hour later and three miles away from the store, I worked up the courage to dart out to the curb where a taxi had just let a passenger off in front of a downtown hotel. The driver did a double take at my sudden appearance in his cab. I hurled myself into the backseat and slid all the way across. After coming to a stop against the armrest, I shrank down and huddled there, trying to make myself invisible to anybody looking in from the street or sidewalk.

It took a few moments to recover enough wind to slink forward and stammer out my home address. The driver, a large man with a full beard, a head meticulously bald enough to make it obvious that he would never consider my products, and putrid breath that caused me to snap my head back quickly to keep its full power from wafting over me, turned and said, "That's a ways from here—you sure you got enough money?"

Disoriented and panting harder than an overheated puppy, I probably came across like an escapee from a locked psychiatric ward who had exhausted himself scaling the fence. I jammed my left hand deep into its corresponding pocket and pulled out a wad of cash.

"Does it look like I have enough of the right presidents here?"

He nodded with approval after a quick glance, "Yep, you do—the only politicians that ever made me happy."

"Are there enough that you'd be willing to wait in my driveway for an hour or so and then run me out to the airport?"

He reached over the seat and picked through the messy fan of bills I held out, "The guy I want to see here wasn't ever a president."

"What, you're looking for counterfeit money?"

"No, I mean Benjamin Franklin. Don't you know your historical facts?"

"Right now they're slipping my mind, I guess."

"Well, you slip me three Benjamins and the whole ride is covered, here to home and home to airport—that even includes the tip," he said, with a magnanimous lilt at the end.

I had to pick through the paper bills clutched in my sweaty fingers to figure out how much he was talking about.

"Three hundred dollars? I'm not asking you to smuggle me across the border. Isn't that a little steep?"

He stroked his beard and looked at me intently.

"It would be for just a ride, but the price includes me keeping my mouth shut, and you look like a guy who values that right about now. Am I right?"

I sighed and handed him the money.

"Close enough."

Thirty minutes later we swung into my driveway.

"I'm going to go in and open the garage door. Do you mind pulling in and waiting there? Just hit the switch to close the door again after you park."

The driver raised his eyebrows and replied, "Okay, but you're not planning anything weird, are you?"

"Well, nothing that involves you."

"That's all I need to know."

BELLY OF THE BEAST

I went through the side entrance, hit the button to open the garage door, and hurried through my house to the dining room I had converted into an office. Once my computer was fired up, it only took a few minutes to get into my foreign accounts and wire almost all of Hair Apparent's cash to them in chunks I had already divvied up. This river of cash was soon followed by a smaller stream from my personal accounts, including the two I had started direct-depositing money into from the phony employees. Hair Apparent had not been in business long enough for it to be a significant amount, but it was there and I did not know how long I would be away or how expensive it would be to maintain myself below the radar.

It took a few more minutes to buy airline tickets and reserve a hotel room, and at the end of it I felt the beginnings of relief at the realization that I was heading south as a rich man with nothing but time on his hands and cash in his pockets. I went downstairs to get my passport, which I kept locked in a safe built into the floor of my basement laboratory.

Gaining access to the safe required that I walk the length of my full-size basement. The stairs brought me first to the room I had sectioned off as the manufacturing heart of Hair Today, a surprisingly compact setup that contained only two pieces of equipment the size of a large and a small furnace, bins of the synthetic carpet pellets that would be processed into fake hair, and shelves covering two walls where the finished goods were stacked. It was after one walked through this room and out into the larger expanse that the scene assumed a strange and disturbing cast, like the lair of a serial sadist.

Arranged with precision along the cinder-block wall was a lineup of upside-down mannequins. Their ankles were lashed with baling wire to pegs protruding from the blocks and their heads soaked in large wooden salad bowls. The liquid stew contained in the bowls looked and smelled like salad that had been left outside over a hot, humid weekend. It was all part of my recent quest to develop a solution that would dissolve the glue that had begun causing so much trouble.

Success had eluded me so far. Most of my efforts, in fact, made things worse. Three nights earlier, for example, a batch that appeared to have been tweaked into a strong contender actually accelerated the contraction process. After taking a break to eat a late dinner and go for a walk, I returned to my lab and found that all four mannequins in my test group had been almost entirely consumed by hairpieces on a hellish mission. The experimental brew gave aggressive life to my hairpieces, which had risen up to consume so much of the dolls that only their feet, were recognizable, still strung to the walls. Hanging below them were bulbous masses of plastic that looked like regurgitated garbage bags held together with plastic cement.

Now I was anxious to see if the new dissolving agent I had hit on the night before had worked on what would have to be my last attempt. That all four experimental subjects were still upside down as I had left them was a good sign, and certainly an easier sight on the eyes than the results of my last fiasco.

I walked over to the closest mannequin.

"C'mon, Maggie, be a good girl for Daddy, okay? Daddy is in trouble and needs to leave in a hurry, so if you could just cooperate and let go of your hair I'd be very grateful. You know I don't like to threaten, but if this doesn't work out, I'm going to have to dress you in 1970s polyester and put you in a window where everybody in the world will see. You don't want that, do you?"

I twisted the baling wire loose and freed Maggie's ankles from the wall. Gently I lifted her by the knees, hesitating to look as her head emerged from the salad bowl out of fear of witnessing another monstrous mutation.

"Let my baby be beautiful," I whispered, in a basement that would muffle a cannon shot.

And this time the result was different. Her head was as smooth and bald as the day I bought her. Left behind to float by itself in the salad bowl was the hairpiece, still in its original benign form. I checked quickly and found that the other three mannequins were similarly bald.

THE GREAT ESCAPE

The final experiment had worked, but before I could celebrate my genius, I sensed a presence in the room. My heart seized up in fear that Al had tracked me down and now stood waiting to wreak horrible revenge. I relaxed a bit when I saw it wasn't Al, but rather Esther and Javier, who had come in to start their day's work and heard me in the lab.

When my feverish eyes lit on them, they clutched each

other's elbows and slowly began shuffling back to the much saner room they had come from.

"Esther, Javier," I called happily, "don't be scared. I know what this looks like . . . well, maybe I don't, but I was doing an experiment with the adhesives and it worked. Sorry for getting carried away like that."

Javier's eyebrows steadily rose as I talked. For a moment I feared some of the bad glue had found its way to his head, but the same eyebrows began heading back down as he spoke.

"Ah, Mr. Adams, do you speak to dolls frequently?"

Still flush with success, I answered, "No, no, only when they cooperate."

"When they what?" The eyebrows shot back up.

"Sorry, I meant to say when the experiment goes well."

"I see." The eyebrows descended a bit. "And what kinds of experiments were you doing?"

"Well, to test the adhesive I had to have them upside down so they would be in the right position to . . ."

Javier grimaced and held up his hands to stop me from continuing.

"Please, sir, say no more. I should not have asked. Forgive me."

Esther jumped in here. "It is good we caught you—I don't mean caught you doing anything bad," she added quickly, "but because we want to show you something."

"Oh, and what is that?" I asked.

"One moment, please," she answered and disappeared into the other room. Esther reappeared seconds later with what looked like a full-length fur coat fit for the wealthiest of the wealthy.

"Where did you get that?"

"Do you remember when Javier showed you what he was working on with artificial fur?"

It had entirely slipped my mind, in fact, but now I recalled.

"Sure, sure, is this what you are trying to make it resemble? If so, you've set the bar awfully high. This is a beautiful piece."

Esther and Javier shook their heads in unison, and then Javier said, "You do not understand. This piece here, it is not real—it is the artificial material."

I reached out and ran my hands over it. Though not an expert on fur, I knew this achieved a standard no fake ever had before.

"Mr. Adams," Esther said as she stepped closer, "normally I would never ask you for a favor, but this, as you can see, is different. Can we try selling our coats in your store?"

I could not risk telling them what was really happening, so I told them that I had to get back to my office for an important meeting. When their faces fell, I added that I would add their request to the meeting agenda, which brightened them right back up.

An idea flashed into my mind and I excused myself to walk back upstairs and call my attorney. Once he heard what I wanted, he assured me it could very easily be done and told me what documents to bring.

Back in the garage, the cab driver had pulled the last few days of the *Wall Street Journal* out of the recycling bin and sat in his cab reading them while public radio news played on the radio.

"Are you studying up on how to invest all the money you're charging me?"

He grinned at that. "Naw, just passing the time."

"Hey, can we make one stop before the airport?"

"Yeah, but what we agreed on . . ."

"I know, I know, how about I give you another one of those Benjamins?"

Slapping the page he was reading for emphasis, the driver said with a broad grin, "Maybe you better throw in a subscription to this newspaper right here—I might just be doing some investing after all."

Despite all I was paying for the trip, I put my own luggage in the trunk and gave the driver directions to my attorney's office. The attorney found my request awfully strange and tried to talk me out of it. I stuck with my plan, though, and emerged half an hour later for the last leg of the journey to the airport.

As the cab moved through traffic, I pulled a lush, jet black hairpiece from the small bag next to me and arranged it on my short-haired, blondish head. Next up was a fake mustache I had toyed with as part of a line of accessories to complement our offerings in the future, along with a pair of sideburns that ended at my jawline. When I looked up, I saw that the driver had adjusted the rearview mirror to watch me.

"Don't ask," I implored.

"Hey, I'm just enjoying the opportunity to watch," he said, his voice making it obvious that he was barely containing a major laughing fit.

I sighed. "Three more Bens keep you from sharing this with anybody?"

"I'll take two if I can watch you put on some chest hair."

Once in the airport I had a few hours to pass before my flight left. I found a corner in a murky cocktail lounge that seemed to offer as much safety as could be found there. It was improbable, I reasoned, for somebody to track me to the airport, but being this close to escaping what would certainly be a harsh fate made it imperative that I take every precaution. When I looked into the mirrored wall to my right, it occurred to me that I looked like an Elvis Presley impersonator with a bad mustache.

When my departure time drew near, I found the men's room

closest to the ticket counter and locked myself into a large stall designated for the handicapped. Off came the hairpiece, mustache, and sideburns, which I cut up with the scissors on my Swiss Army knife and then flushed down the toilet. Then I took off my clothes and changed into another set from my bag. I wadded the old clothes up into a ball, with the knife at the center, and threw them in the garbage bin on the way out.

Emerging from the restroom, I felt naked and exposed, but my face had to match the picture on my license if I wanted to board the plane. After a quick detour to the cocktail lounge for a couple more shots of Wild Turkey, I threw a couple of breath mints into my mouth and headed for the ticket counter.

Thirteen

A FLOUNDER IN PARADISE

Possibility never disappoints; wealth does.

S ir, please, you must wake up, you're shouting in your sleep and disturbing the other passengers. Sir, I'm going to have to call the captain if you don't stop immediately."

Between the stewardess's urgent whispering in my ear and her fingernails digging into my shoulder when she shook it with both hands, I was driven from my nightmare and woke up and immediately stopped ranting. The stewardess remained planted at my side for a few more moments, as if fearing I would go back to sleep the moment she turned her back and resume disrupting all the A-list people on the flight.

Exhausted from the stress of recent events, which included a few too many Wild Turkeys in the airport cocktail lounge, I had conked out the second my flight to Mexico City became airborne. I had sprung for first class and the seat was too comfortable for me to stay awake for long. Apparently I slept soundly for the first couple of hours, but then the nightmare came upon me. It began with me finding myself trapped in Hair Apparent's storeroom. Dozens of customers were converging on me, howling in pain and bloodlust, their arms held straight out with fingers straining for my throat. My hairpieces were perched on every head and the synthetic monstrosities had stripped the flesh from all of their faces, leaving them without eyelids or any recognizable features—just muscle and blood on bone. I ran into the employee bathroom, slammed the door shut, and locked it. Just as I turned toward a small window I prayed was big enough to squeeze through, zombie hands burst through all four walls.

A quick scan of my fellow passengers revealed none of them to be hairpiece zombies, though many looked irritated enough to go for my throat if I kept up the shouting.

"Thanks, miss, I'm okay now. I just had a bad dream, that's all."

"You sure you're okay?" she asked, her eyes probing mine for glimmers of sanity.

"Yes, yes, I am," I replied, my voice still a little shaky. "Oh, miss?" I added as she started down the aisle, "Could I have a double shot of whatever kind of scotch is closest?"

A STRANGER IN STRANGE COMPANY

Three double shots later, plus a couple more I bribed the lady next to me to order on my behalf, I wobbled off the plane and into the Mexico City airport. Though not at my most clearheaded, I knew better than to check into a hotel reserved under my real name, but what path should I follow instead? Forty-five minutes later the answer arrived in the form of a noisy group of college kids bursting into the coffee shop where I was downing shots of espresso in a doomed attempt to jump-start my powers of reason.

In loud, angry voices they revealed that a small tour bus chartered for a sightseeing tour that would get them to Cancun in time for spring break was in danger of being lost, along with their deposit, if they could not come up with enough money to cover the cost of five friends who had changed their minds at the last minute.

Why not?

I stood up, steadied myself against the sudden whirl of lights, and walked over with the caution of a wiley drunk taking a sobriety test.

"I'll go," I slurred.

"Huh?" the nearest one, who appeared to be their leader answered. "Who are you?"

"Look, I know I'm about a dozen years older than the rest of you, but I never had the chance to go to Cancun when I was in college, and I just had an investment of mine pay off big time."

That grabbed their attention and the kids looked at each other uncertainly. Left to itself, this process was not going to resolve in my favor. The greed I knew would have worked on me at that age had less power over this group.

"Here's the deal. I heard somebody mention that five members of your party bailed out and now you guys are short the money you need, which means you won't get to Cancun. I'll pay for all five spots, cash, and promise not to get in anybody's way the whole trip. We okay to roll?"

And so the deal was sealed and I spent the next four days traveling with a group of college juniors and seniors. They were a lot more interested in having pictures taken of themselves drunk at different historic locations than in learning anything about the sites. From the city of Puebla to the Chichen Itza ruins to the Caribbean coast, the kids acted out recycled reality television scripts and produced a slew of what looked like bad lite beer advertisements: phone photos with beer cans front and center and history as a blurry backdrop.

My plan was to separate from them as quickly as possible

once we got to Cancun, but I underestimated the significance
of spring break, an occasion that meant there were no single
rooms available. Fortunately, my new college buddies had rented
a villa and just happened to need somebody to take up the
slack left by the five friends who had forsaken them. Naturally
I paid for all five, on the condition that I get a private room of
my choice.

BROODING BELOW THE BORDER

The Cancun beaches were beautiful and the villa was a lot
nicer than anything I expected college kids to get. My room was
airy and big, with a Jacuzzi and a balcony that gave me a wonderful view of the gulf. The facility had great food and drinks,
and the second the staff saw that I tipped much more generously than spring breakers, the service became top notch.

I spent a lot of time watching cable news in my room. The
story of my homicidal hairpieces was treated as a curiosity, and
everybody reporting on it had serious doubts about its truth.
Most concluded that bad plastic surgery, done in conjunction
with buying the hairpieces in a pathetic effort to appear youthful, was the real problem. No mention was made of my fleeing
the country or looting Hair Apparent.

I called my attorney to see what he knew.

"Luke, where are you? Do you have any idea how many angry people are looking for you?" he asked in a hoarse whisper.

"Bill, why are you whispering? Is somebody there with you?"

"No, no, I'm on my cell in a restaurant and don't want anybody to hear."

A little spooked, I told him, "Look, I took a little vacation and was wondering if I should come back or just stay away. You get my drift?"

"Sure, sure," he answered. "Look, I'm not going to lie. Al and your other partner and all the investors are furious and would love to string you up. You took every dollar and the store is shut down, not to mention checks bouncing like crazy and creditors demanding answers that nobody has."

"So I guess this vacation should maybe become permanent?"

"Not necessarily. You see, Luke, this Hair Apparent gold mine can still pull in a fortune and everybody involved knows that, but without you it becomes a dry hole. To cut to the chase, so to speak, you come back and there won't be any charges—so long as you return the money. You can even go back to your old job, with some pretty close supervision, of course."

"No arrest, no jail, no nothing like that?"

"Right, my boy. Even when the golden goose has been naughty, killing it doesn't do anybody any good."

"So long as the golden eggs keep rolling along, right?"

"Right. I guess you haven't lost your mind after all."

At first the idea of going back had no appeal. I was in paradise and could afford to stay put a long time if I wanted to. For the next week I made the most of it; partying late into the night, sleeping in, lying on the beach, eating and drinking like a king, making new friends, and not doing a single thing I didn't want to. Two days into it I was miserable.

It made no sense. Everything was perfect and I should have been ecstatic, but I felt worse than at any other time in my life. What was eating at me so badly? My conscience—a thing I thought had gone on permanent vacation long ago. Even though I had millions of dollars at my fingertips, it decided to wake up now and make me feel worse than worthless.

FROM DOLLARS TO DOLDRUMS

One afternoon, when everybody else in the villa was out getting an early start on Happy Hour, I set out to account for how I felt. As a starting point I began with the total dollars I had available. My own rightful money did not amount to much, so I used what I had stolen. Between the investors' funds, the bank loan, and a few smaller items, it came to $8,129,500.

But how to attach a dollar amount to how bad I felt? In psychological and spiritual terms no positive thoughts or feelings were present, so any positive numbers were out. Zero was too high, because at that point I would feel neutral. So a negative amount made sense, but how negative? Well, as near as I could tell, it seemed that I felt about like I would if I owed $8,129,500 instead of being able to spend it as I pleased. In other words, I had a negative $8,129,500 weighing me down. To restore myself, I would have to return the stolen money and add the same amount of value to the company to work back to a positive $8,129,500. A 100 percent penalty had been imposed on me—by me!

At the time I did not understand how closely heavenly accounting resembled karma, with a strong Old Testament twist. But it did occur to me that if I was hitting myself with a 100 percent penalty immediately, there would surely be hell to pay with interest if I didn't begin working off the fine quickly.

Here is how my outstanding debt looked to me.

THE RECKONING, PART 1

FAT (Funds Available from Theft)

Balance	$ 8,129,500
100% Penalty	8,129,500
CAD (Conscience Assessment Due)	$ 16,259,000

Imagine that, a few days earlier I didn't think my conscience had any muscle, and now it was turning out to be more brutal than any loan shark.

Just how brutal? What had only been a small, usually silent voice within brought up the fact that in addition to stealing from Hair Apparent in the present, I had also stolen from its future by causing it to shut down and ruining the firm's reputation. We know that the net worth of the business on paper was $320,000. That, however, is the value in strict accounting terms, and these only go by objective amounts that follow strict rules. The actual market value is better judged by what outsiders were willing to pay for the business. We saw that in the investors' second offer of $15,170,00.

The small voice with the rapidly increasing volume went on to inform me that it didn't stop there. The investors planned on making a lot of money and must have been very optimistic in their profit projections. Just how much so? I thought I remembered from a college finance class that the historical average rate of return on investment for American firms was around 12 percent annually. The investors thought they were going to do much, much better than this, but, I reasoned, accomplishing and maintaining the goal would be easier said than done.

Because I was feeling so bad about myself, I settled on a 20 percent annual return on their investment (purchase price of Hair Apparent) that we could have earned if I had talked Al into selling instead of stealing everything and heading south. To get an idea of the future value of investments accountants use future value tables that enable them to estimate what an amount will grow to over different periods of time.

For example, let's say we had accepted the investors' second offer and I invested $100,000 of my share in an account for the next ten years, earning 9 percent compound interest a year. In ten years it would grow to $1,519,293. Say the account did a lot better and earned 15 percent annually; then it would come in at $2,303,718. And if things went the other way, say, 5 percent? Then the result would be $1,257,789.

Over time the effect of compounding interest builds. To illustrate, if we go back to the original $100,000 a year invested at 9 percent and extend it to twenty years, our money grows to a whopping $5,116,012. You can see where this is going: in the worlds of finance and conscience, letting things ride for years has a multiplier effect.

Below is my hotel room estimate of that effect. It assumes a return, or fine, on what my conscience told me I owed, plus the value I had stolen. The fine would be levied every year and get steeper every year due to compounding.

THE RECKONING, PART 2: BIGGER AND BADDER

CAD (Conscience Assessment Due)	$ 16,259,000
TOT (Theft of Tomorrow)	15,170,000
ROT (Reckoning's Ongoing Total)	$ 31,429,000
	×20
20% Annual Fine on ROT	$ 6,285,800
Future Value Factor	×187
DAFT (Debt Accumulated for Tomorrow)	$1,173,483,428

These calculations went a long way toward explaining why I felt so badly. My choice was clear: I could return and spend years working off a huge debt, or I could live well off the money I'd stolen for however many years I had left, and then face a vastly steeper price tag when the inevitable reckoning came.

Fourteen

TO FALL WITHOUT GRACE

*Flying too high for your own little sky guarantees
a hard landing.*

A few days after my calculating frenzy, spring break ended
and my new friends went back to school. I, on the other
hand, had decided to return home and face what was
sure to be some very unpleasant music. But maybe not immediately. Not long before my conscience struck, I used one of the
college kids' laptops to reserve a room for a week at a beautiful
hotel in Rio de Janeiro. The room reservation came with a discount for a nearby hang-gliding school. The promotional materials promised to take any client from a fear of heights to solo
flights in a few short days.

On television, hang-gliding had always looked like fun to me,
so why not give it a try while I still could? Once I put that hair
shirt and yoke back on at Hair Apparent, there wouldn't be va-
cations anytime soon. I called my lawyer and told him to expect
me in a week.

"A week—you really are insane," he bellowed. "You'll get a
break if you get back here pronto, but all bets might be off if you
drag your heels too much."

"One week, Bill. Tell Al and the boys I'll come back rested

and fully charged up, and ready to crank out enough hair to cover every bald head that can afford it."

I hung up on Bill's sputtering and prepared to leave.

A SOUTHERN EXPOSURE

My instruction went very well the first two days and I could hardly wait for day 3, the first opportunity those who qualified could make a solo flight. Nothing too risky, just taking off from a platform on a mountain overlook and riding the breeze down to a gentle landing on the white ocean sands below. By the time I went out alone I had flown the same route with an instructor a few times and had progressed to where I could do everything on my own under the instructor's supervision.

As I prepared for my solo outing on a bright, clear morning perfect for hang-gliding, a mysterious figure shuffled up to join the group of fellow students observing my efforts. It was a man, but his face wasn't visible because he wore what looked like a badly fitting monk's robe with the cowl pulled over his face. Something about his presence disturbed me.

"Do you know who that is?" I whispered to the instructor, giving a slight head nod to indicate who I meant. The instructor glanced over and dismissed my concerns with a small wave of his hand.

"Nothing to worry about, sir, he's just a homeless beggar. They're everywhere and see tourists as good marks."

I'd heard about the huge garbage dumps ringing Rio and how they were populated by desperately poor people in search of any scrap of food or useful article. It sounded like a reasonable explanation, but something about the beggar seemed familiar. I shook off the sensation, though, because it was time to finalize preparations for my first solo flight.

THE SEA REFUSES NO GIVER

As I took off, a voice behind me shouted, "Hey, Luke!" This startled me badly because nobody here should have known my real name. I twisted my neck and looked back. The beggar's cowl was off now and he glared at me with blazing, angry eyes. The sun shone off his bald head, but even through the glare and widening distance I could see his face, really nothing more than folds of flesh that cascaded off his forehead and drooped almost to his chest, a look that would make a basset hound beg for a facelift.

Now the man cupped his hands on either side of his mouth to up the volume, "You like sixties music, right? Well, instant karma's about to get you!"

The music geek in my head automatically provided a silent response, "Wait a second, the song wasn't released until . . ." but the thought was cut off by a sudden cracking sound and the sight of my left wing breaking off and flying into space. Suddenly I began spinning wildly to that side and heading toward a thicket of boulders that bordered the beach I was supposed to land on. At the last second I steadied my right wing enough that it caught an updraft. This flipped me out past the boulders and into the ocean.

Though better than being splattered on the rocky shoals, I found myself in a rip current carrying me out to sea, fast. I was so badly tangled in the ruined hang-glider—the seat belt still clung to me—that there was no way to resist the flow. Just as I finally freed myself from the seat belt and shed the remains of the hang-glider I noticed that the current was bringing me into the midst of a group of fishing trawlers. Instantly I began waving my arms and yelling to attract attention. A few minutes later I was near the side of one boat and my spirits soared. I was going to make it!

The next thing I knew I was being swept up into the air atop a huge gaggle of sparkling, wriggling fish. It came to me: I had been caught in a fishing net. Well, at least that would get me on board. As the net was hauled up into the air and over the side of the boat, I slid down into the midst of the desperately squirming fish and felt a sharp sting on my side. I looked down and saw that a small jellyfish had attached itself to my hip. It felt like I had been lathered up with Agent Orange. As I reached to pry the thing off, a much bigger jellyfish settled on top of my head. The new sensation was like being screwed into a giant light socket. The last thing that flashed through my mind was the video of John Lennon recording *Instant Karma* in 1970.

Fifteen

A RUEFUL REUNION

Nothing is harder to scale than a mountain of compounding karmic debt.

During my purgatory project, many, many hours were devoted to scribbling on legal pads with pencils. Computers were not allowed, not even typewriters. In a little classroom I sat hunched over my postage stamp–sized desktop in a tiny, rickety chair that always seemed to be on the verge of complete collapse. Leg cramps plagued me because I couldn't help but try to keep my weight off it.

Whenever I filled up a pad or wore a pencil down to the nub, I pried my rear end out of the chair and walked to the front of the classroom. There the article had to be placed in a bin on the teacher's desk. The adult desk was a large, fancy affair, with a very comfortable-looking chair. Using either was strictly forbidden.

Once I turned in the full pad or pencil stub, I would return to my seat, lift up the desktop, and take another from the neatly arranged supplies within. The pencil sharpener was in the back, mounted on the wall next to the boy's room. When a pencil became dull, I could not simply take another. Somehow the desk knew and locked itself. I had to get up, which meant pushing the miniature chair back far enough to extract my legs from below the desk so that I did not stand and topple it, and go use the sharpener. Some of the most aggravating moments came when I got myself situated again—not easy when one is squeezing into a kindergarten-sized space and trying to avoid banging shins that have already been scraped raw, only to witness the pencil point breaking before the first sentence is completed.

On this particular day something much more disturbing happened. I was particularly intent on finishing a page before my lunch break, which always meant a peanut butter and jelly sandwich on spongy white bread with a carton of 1 percent milk and a single serving bag of crushed potato chips to be eaten at my doll desk, when I heard a rustling noise from the front of the room. I raised my head and saw Al sitting there looking at me with a neutral expression on his face. It was the Al from before the hairpiece, complete with the bad old comb-over.

I rose up instantly and sent the desk and chair flying. Badly frightened, I followed my instinct to take flight, which meant running out the classroom door. In doing that I forgot how low the opening was and smacked my forehead on an iron-hard piece of wood trim. I came to, with Al kneeling down beside me. I had a headache that seemed unfairly painful, considering that I was already dead.

INSTANT KARMA'S AFTERMATH

"So we all really do shine on, huh, Luke?"

Too dizzy to stand, I used my feet to push myself away from Al and scooted across the linoleum until I came to a stop with my shoulders squeezed into a child's coat cubby.

Al shook his head and laughed quietly.

"Don't worry, Luke, I'm not after you now. I already killed you once, and now I'm dead, too."

"Wha . . . ? How . . . ?" I stammered, still groggy from the blow to my head.

"Look, you're not hard to find, be it on Earth or here in the afterlife. After you ditched me that day in the store, I immediately called a private detective I'd used before, and he was waiting down the street from your house before you got there. After that, following you to the airport, then tracking you across Mexico and into Brazil didn't give him any problems."

"So, what, he was the weird-looking guy I saw before I went off the cliff? He followed me there?" I asked, struggling to piece things together in the fog.

"He was there, all right, but the guy in the robe who yelled to you when you took off in the hang-glider in Rio? That was me. The night before your solo flight I told the owner I wanted to know which hang-glider you'd be using so that a photographer friend of ours down on the beach could be sure to film you. Once I slipped him a few bucks, he had no problem with it. From there all I had to do was weaken a wing enough so that it would snap once it was under enough stress, not hard to do with my construction background."

Still catching up to the narrative, I said, "That was you? But, but, I didn't recognize you."

"Well, remember, you e-mailed the recipe for the dissolving solution to the store? I used it and it worked—the hairpiece came off."

Al paused and then snapped his fingers. "By the way, was it really necessary to stand on my head and soak in a salad bowl? I did it because I was afraid not to."

A mental picture of a portly Al upside down with the top of his skull marinating made a smile tug at the corners of my mouth.

"No, probably not, but I didn't have time to change what seemed to work. Sorry about that."

He shrugged and continued. "Anyway, that hairpiece from hell had ratcheted my face so tight that when it relaxed I had enough loose skin to cover a few more heads with, which is why you didn't recognize me."

"And now you're dead, too?"

"Yeah, when I got back and was searching your house some more, I ran into Javier and Esther—a nice couple, by the way—and brought them up to speed. Once they found out I was a partner, they showed me the imitation furs they were making in your basement. Since the store was already there, I figured why not? So we switched over to their products, fur coats, fur-trimmed boots, and so on. A few days into it some animal rights guy who didn't know the stuff was fake came into the store and threw some kind of animal blood all over me. I chased him outside, and right before I wrapped my hands around his throat, I slipped on some of the blood and fell. My head hit the curb and that's all she wrote."

Still playing catch-up, my mind had just processed his confession.

"Hang on, you say you made the hang-glider go down? I . . . I thought it was an accident, something on the wing just broke."

"The wing did break," Al agreed, "but it was no accident."

I let the details sink in.

"You know, my running from the country and leaving the rest of you to deal with the mess was no accident either, so I guess I can't be too mad about your booby-trapping the wing. I figured you'd want to come after me. I just thought I'd gotten away clean."

"It's pretty hard to get away clean when you've made that kind of mess."

Slowly, so as not to make the pain in my head worse, I nodded in agreement.

"I know you won't believe this, but I was going to come back and try to make things right after my trip to Rio."

Al looked at me quizzically. "And you don't think there would have been more trips to make and places to see if you hadn't died?"

"No, no, of course not . . . but now that I think about it, the time line could have gotten stretched out a bit more, I guess."

Al nodded to himself. "Just like I thought."

"But I would have returned," I insisted. "After all I stole, between the money and Hair Apparent's future, I had to start working off . . ."

"Nothing," Al interjected.

"Come again?"

"Our investors got a load of those furs Esther and Javier were making with your equipment and bought them out immediately, lock, stock, and barrel. The two of them made a fortune and will earn even more running the operation for us. Everybody agreed that you actually did them a favor by taking off, even if you never returned the money."

"They didn't want me back?" I asked in disbelief.

Al laughed at that. "Sure, to buy a fake fur coat. The new process has so many applications, from coats to cars, it makes your hairpieces look like small potatoes."

JOURNEY TO THE CENTER OF OUR SOULS

Al squeezed into the coat cubby next to mine and we spent some more time getting caught up. Once my head cleared and I got used to the idea of my venture being eclipsed, new questions began to rush in.

"Al, if you're dead, shouldn't you have been sent to Heaven or Hell by now? Why are you still here?"

"Luke, my boy, I've been placed in Purgatory along with you. Believe it or not, it seemed that my life had pointed me toward Heaven, but then I killed you. Normally, murder gets you into Hell with no appeal, but it was obvious that, what with the hairpiece eating me alive and our company going down the tubes, I wasn't in my right mind."

"So how is your fate going to be decided?"

"There's the rub. You and I have a couple of days to sort of work that out. We're scheduled to give a presentation, in fact."

The news sent me into an immediate panic.

"No, that can't be. I'm supposed to be writing an accounting guide for AudiTrix and I'm nowhere near done. All I've finished so far is my own story and covered some basic accounting stuff, and they haven't even given me the new standards they've developed so I can explain. . . ."

Al reached around and took a firm hold of my forearm.

"Get a grip, son—the plan has changed. AudiTrix is finishing up the training for the first graduating class of HAPs and we're their capstone project."

"What?"

"That's right," Al replied, and gave a firm nod to emphasize the point, "You and I have got to sit here, nose to nose, and hammer out a document that they have to evaluate and score as part of credential testing. It's called a SOW, which stands for Statement of Worth."

"But we don't know anything about the new standards," I protested.

"We do now—look."

Al pointed to a pair of loose-leaf binders that had appeared on the teacher's desk.

"What are those?"

"Those are copies of the same standards the HAPs have to go by when they judge us. Applying the standards is part of that project; they call it the Final Accounting Reasoning Test."

I mulled that over a bit and then said, "Hey, Al, if you put together the letters of those words you come up with . . ."

"Yeah, yeah, I know," he interrupted. "It stinks."

EVERYDAY I WRITE THE BOOK

I went over my copy quickly in hopes of containing the anxiety that began building when I learned from Al that my assignment had changed. The gist of the standards and how they were to be applied was pretty straightforward: with Earth being used as a test site for a judgment methodology that would be applied to the entire universe, the goal was merely to get a general idea if the standards were workable and efficient or not. They would be tested on Al and me and a cluster of other recently deceased earthlings. Humans are among the simplest of the universe's species to be judged. We were to be the experimental fruit flies of our galaxy.

Instead of dollars, heavenly accounting dictates that karma koins be used as currency. For humans it is okay to write them like dollars or any other of the world's forms of money for the sake of understandability, but they are very different. When a human action is stated in karma koins, three factors come into play. First, there is an estimate made of how good or bad the action was. An action or set of actions that cause the world or any part of it to become better, like being a loving mother, also cause karma koins to increase, similar to the way revenues increase when a business is successful. Causing the world to be-come worse off is treated like an expense, a sacrifice of limited resources to be subtracted according to how negative the action was. An example of something that would be a karmic subtraction is selling a used car with the knowledge that the brakes are about to give out and not saying anything about it.

The second part of karmic valuation is much trickier. It is based on estimates of the future impact our actions have, the ways in which the "gifts" we give keep on giving. For example, a loving mother who raises a happy child who then becomes a productive, compassionate adult is richly rewarded with glittering flows of karma koins. A bad parent who raises a miserable human being who then goes forth to spread the affliction discovers that the heavy karma koin deductions make his or her misdeeds very expensive. On the other hand, going back to the used car example, if the brakes are repaired and nothing terrible happens, the karmic deductions are nowhere near as bad as if the brakes fail and a thruway pileup results.

The third aspect is based on what is in our hearts when we act. This means that our intentions are measured. Did we want to do something decent, or were we out to do harm, or did we simply not care? Lots of things can happen between the spark that leads us to act and how that act pans out. What if someone is a wonderful parent, but a child grows up to become a criminal anyway? Or what if someone is an abusive parent and the child, despite that background, evolves into a kind, generous person?

Accounting as practiced on Earth, of course, has a much narrower scope. It has no way of knowing what lurks in the hearts of men and cannot track the impact of a decision very far into the future. Only what can be observed, measured, and verified is allowed into accounting systems, and that is as it should be. Heavenly accounting can do more because it has access to so much more information. Heavenly auditing professionals—HAPs—have been given access by the Almighty to everything an individual has ever done and thought. Indeed, Big Brother watches us in ways we never imagined.

Having every nasty deed, especially those you thought had gone unobserved, broadcast like a Hollywood feature film and your every secret thought played with crystal clear audio is a jarring experience. Especially when you have to answer for them.

Sixteen

THE ETERNALLY CHALLENGED

From those to whom much has been given much more must be given back.

We spent most of the morning in silence, going through our loose-leaf binders in detail. One procedure that seemed similar to a concept I remembered from college accounting struck me and I disturbed the studious air with a question.

"Hey, Al, do you get this business on SLAP here in section 12?"

"I think so. I read through it a little bit ago; it stands for Spread Levied According to Personality, right?"

"Yes, but I'm not real clear on it."

"Do you remember doing present-value calculations back in college? I still do and I'm older than you."

"That," I answered, "is because you went to college before calculators were invented and it took a long time."

What I remembered about present value is that it was a tool for taking cash to be received in the future and restating it in today's dollars. Present value, according to the memory jog that the binder provided, does this with discount rates. These reflect the risk, the uncertainty, and the opportunity costs of those future cash flows. The greater these are, the higher the discount rate and the lower the present value.

Say, for example, you are going to receive $1,000 in five years and somebody offers you the chance to get paid today instead. Naturally, you would be willing to take less than the $1,000 to have use of the money now, but how much less? What if you thought there was a significant risk (the probability of something adverse happening) of not receiving the money? What if it was highly uncertain (meaning difficult to predict) that you would get the money or there were good opportunities you could pursue if you got the money right now? How much less than $1,000 would you take—$900, $750, $500? These amounts are arrived at according to the discount taken, and the more risk, uncertainty, and opportunity costs there are, the bigger the discount. The higher the discount rate used, the more is lopped off that $1,000 and the less you get today. If the risks, uncertainty, and opportunity costs are less, then a lower discount rate is used, fewer dollars are lopped off, and you get more today.

All of that I understood. It was the AudiTrix spin on it that confused me.

"Okay, Al, I get present value and karma koins are starting to make sense, but what's this business with different present values and a spread?"

Al paused to rub the expanse of bare skin on top of his skull and answered, "It looks like people who are born with lots of ability and grow up in good situations are expected to give more back if they want to make it to Heaven. After the good things they do are valued in karma koins, a higher discount rate than most other people get is applied. This means they have to really go the distance to wind up with a respectable present value. But at the same time, the resources they use up and the bad things they do, which are lumped together as costs for some reason, get discounted at a lower rate."

"Which means what?"

"Well, it seems to boil down to the fact that those most blessed in life don't catch a break when they mess up. They are heavily penalized and have to work twice as hard as everybody else to cover the costs. I think that's it, anyway."

"And your thinking is essentially correct, though somewhat muddled."

Our heads snapped around at the voice coming from the front of the classroom. There before us sat a man who, from the wingtips visible beneath the desk to the swept-back shock of gray hair glistening below the fluorescent lights, looked like he had been created at central casting to play a law school professor on a television series. He had rigid posture, a brow borrowed from George Washington, and glittering hawklike eyes and was clad in a black suit offset by a starched white shirt and burgundy tie. With his bifocals perched on his roman nose—the better to look down on us—and the facial expression of one who gargles with lemon juice even though he hates it, this gentleman radiated superior intellect and authority.

"Who are you?" we asked in unison.

Rearing back slightly, our visitor introduced himself. "My name is Eldridge Franklin Hutton and I am the CSI, which, I am sure you know, stands for central scrutinizer incarnate."

I replied, "You've got to be kidding! Isn't that from a Frank Zappa song?" After all the unbelievable things I had been through, it seems silly to have said this.

"Should Mr. Zappa have borrowed the phrase, it hardly matters to our current pursuit. I have been commissioned to see that you view all relevant material and understand the relationships between the actions you selected during life and their corresponding karma koin valuations and present-value determinations."

Al and I looked at each other. Then Al shrugged and asked our new CSI, "So I'm on track with the discount rates?"

"You are as close as one so recently deceased can get, I suppose," Mr. Hutton answered, and cleared his throat before proceeding. "The first number the heavenly auditing professionals will have to settle on is the BAD."

"Wait a second, isn't using bad numbers what got me into all this trouble?" I asked.

EF, as I was already beginning to label Mr. Hutton, looked at me and let out a short sigh.

"Mr. Adams, BAD stands for Blessing-Adjusted Discount. It is the amount by which your karma koin present value is reduced. As Mr. Borland stated, the more advantages you experienced in life, the larger the rate assigned."

"Sort of like a golf handicap?"

"It distresses me to think that a similarity exists with a sport whose participants dress so hideously, but yes, I suppose the underlying idea is similar."

Encouraged by my perceptiveness, I added, "So the purpose is to level the playing field, then?"

EF shook his head impatiently.

"The idea is to give those less abundantly blessed the opportunity to be rewarded for making the most of their limited resources, an admirable effort we intend to continue encouraging."

"But is that fair?"

"I have no doubt you will find it so when applied to your case. You see, Mr. Adams, considering that your parents abandoned you as a young child to an unstable uncle while they pursued their dream of rock-and-roll fame gives you an advantage."

Al looked at me with raised eyebrows. "I didn't know any of this."

I shrugged and told him, "Mom and Dad left to tour with a

heavy-metal band called Karkus when I was in first grade. They thought the group was going to be huge, but they ended up playing frat parties and bar mitzvahs and I never heard from them again. Uncle Kenny was convinced they'd been abducted by aliens, and his state of mind never got better."

"Is he still around?"

"No, he died when I was in high school. He was trying to drown voices in the radio; he thought they were making fun of him. Unfortunately, it was still plugged in when he held it under the kitchen faucet."

Al just looked at me.

EF paused to give Al a chance to get his jaws working again and then went on. "Given your difficult circumstances, we will be using a low discount rate to value your good deeds, which means their present value will be maximized. At the same time, because it is obvious that somebody with your upbringing and experiences is unlikely to possess sound judgment as an adult, the negative things you did will be discounted at a high rate. This means their present value will be minimized."

"Wow, so that means I've got a real shot at getting out of here and moving up?"

EF gazed at me severely.

"I've conducted a preliminary review of many of the events that led to your coming here, and they do not form a pretty picture. Even with a generous net present-value calculation and assuming the written work you have produced here is adequate, the final decision is certain to be a very close one."

"Now then," EF called out crisply with a clap of his hands, "I am going to the board to give you some additional insight into BAD SLAP, beginning with a review of how discount rates are used in earthly accounting. From the looks on your faces and the way your lips moved while reading the materials, I surmise that you are both in need of remediation and some handholding—figuratively speaking, of course.

WHEN BLACK FRIDAY COMES

"We'll begin with a review of how the present value of future cash flows is calculated. Because Mr. Borland's explanation of a few minutes ago was essentially correct, let us proceed directly to some examples. Open your binders to page ninety-eight."

I did so and saw nothing but the table below on the page:

PRESENT VALUE OF AN ANNUITY
Discount Rate:
Number of Time Periods:
Payment Amount:
Present Value:

EF went on to direct us. "As you know, the greater the factors of risk, uncertainty, and opportunity cost, the higher the discount rate. To illustrate, let us say you are going to receive $15,000 a year for twenty years. Calculate the present value of these cash flows with a low discount rate, say, 8 percent, which means there is not much risk and so on, and then at a higher rate, 20 percent in this case, to reflect significantly more risk and uncertainty. What are the present values of each?"

I looked down at my blank page and flipped through the surrounding pages in search of tables that provided discount rates. There were none to be found; nor were any calculators in sight. I hated to ask, but it was a better alternative that sitting there with my mind firing blanks.

"Excuse me, Mr. Hutton, but we don't have anything to solve the problem with."

"You most certainly do, right in front of you. Just enter the numbers next to the appropriate entries," EF answered, as though speaking to a student with a serious head injury.

"Okay, but . . ." I entered the discount rate, number of years, and dollar amount per year where EF told me to, and before I lifted my pencil from the paper, the present value using 8 percent appeared: $147,272.21. Then I did the same at 20 percent and it appeared, too: $73,043.70. I looked up at the board where EF stood and saw that he had written the answers without the benefit of a calculator, computer, or answer key.

"You don't need a calculator? You figured the answers out in your head?"

"I do not need to move my lips when I read, either," EF answered, sounding awfully haughty about it. Returning to our lesson, he continued. "With both discount rates you are calculating the value in today's dollars of the $300,000 to be received over twenty years. The more risk and uncertainty there is, as with the 20 percent rate, the less it is worth to you today."

"How does this relate to deciding if people are going to Heaven or Hell?" I asked.

"AudiTrix has developed a twofold process to determine a judgee's net present value. First, it values what the judgee did in life, stating the value in karma koins. A karma koin is a unit of measure for the intent of an individual's actions and the impact they have on others. Good intentions and results that benefit the surrounding world are stated in positive numbers of karma koins, much the way earthlings use currencies to display increases in income. Bad intentions and poor outcomes that leave the surrounding world worse off are combined with the resources used up during life and stated in negative numbers of karma koins, as earthlings use currencies to display expenses."

"Okay, I think I get that part of it, but where does the present value come in?"

"A good question, Mr. Adams, which is a welcome relief. After one dies, the deeds of a lifetime continue to have an impact on the planet. Consider: not only do beings affect those they interact with initially, they also influence how those beings treat others and how these groups go on to act. To understand the effect, think of a rock dropped into a pond and how far the ripples generated go."

"That means . . ." I began, and let the unformed thought trail off.

"That means bad actors sink like stones when Judgment Day comes."

Al chimed in with, "So this is where present value comes in?"

EF snapped his fingers at gunshot volume and pointed at Al. "Very good, Mr. Borland. The length of time and magnitude of impact over those years varies greatly from person to person, but it seems that preliminary results show one hundred years to be a good starting point. Adjustments can be made from there according to the life being examined. So, you see, we have future flows of karma koins that are discounted and then added to the karmic valuations of the life recently completed. This gives us a net present value."

Al, who was on a roll and blatantly courting EF's favor, said, "So a positive net present value means that a person has done more good than harm and can go to Heaven?"

"Exactly, my shining light of a student, and a negative net present value means that one can only hope the judgee enjoyed warm weather during life."

With that, EF's eyes locked on mine and he grinned wickedly.

"I believe, Mr. Adams, that you were seeking warmer climates when you fled the country after looting your company, correct?"

"Well, this isn't the place to lie about it, I guess, so, yes, you are correct," I replied, with a powerful feeling of dread swelling within me.

"It is time, then, to find out how it all comes out in the wash for you, Mr. Adams. You are about to sort through a lifetime and more of dirty laundry, with Mr. Borland's assistance."

"Gentlemen, hold your noses."

Seventeen

EXERCISE OF A LIFETIME

Do not worship the ground that awaits you.

S
o far I had only meager resources to work with: pencils, pads, a 1950s era school library down the hall, and a dial-up modem at the mercy of a Purgatory party line. This bare-bones arrangement changed in a flash. Suddenly top-of-the-line computers and monitors surrounded us. Not only did we have instant Internet access, we could also click on to a site ages beyond anything available on Earth.

EternaTube allowed users to search for any time, event, location, or person from their lives on Earth. A menu of clips with descriptions would pop up on the screen. An even more astounding feature made it possible to enter any action or decision and see the effects it had on other people far into the future. Many of them I had never met during life. Many had not been born yet.

The wonders did not end here. Holographic time lines running the lengths of the walls tracked my life from birth to that final trek to Brazil. Significant happenings and milestones were highlighted, and I could watch these episodes in detail simply by pushing a button. They were like movies in midair.

Al quickly became distracted by the power to call up embarrassing episodes from my teenage years, and even EF snickered at these. I detoured off into seeing how much money could be made in the future by picking different stocks in the present, though my being dead only caused the knowledge to frustrate me. It was time to join forces with Al for the morbid task of valuing the mess I had made with my life.

EF gave us five days for the job and directed us to the sections in our binders, which had swelled many sizes, that contained instructions for how to value actions and their repercussions in karma koins. At first, the process intimidated me because it sounded incredibly complicated, but it wasn't. A surprising amount of room for individual interpretation and estimation was built in, and it didn't take long for us to develop a system wherein karma koin amounts were determined by the episode. This included what we called sequels: future repercussions, whether positive or negative, stemming from the original event. It was like tracing a threaded discussion on a blog, and we quickly got the hang of it.

For example, one of my rare good deeds had been to volunteer at a veterans' hospital during college (actually I had to as part of the community service requirement following a disorderly conduct arrest, but I did keep going a little longer on my own). EternaTube showed me visiting with the veterans, helping them sort mail, taking them for walks, and a bunch of other nice things. Then we followed the "threads" to see the impact on the veterans and their families, friends, and the staff during this time period and beyond. One vet's granddaughter even named a baby after me! Proof of my kind heart being played before us made my chest swell with pride.

"I'd give this 110 karma koins for the volunteering done in college, plus another 40 annually for the positive fallout over the next sixty-five years," Al called out a bit after we completed our incident review.

"What?" I replied indignantly, "Didn't you see how their faces lit up when I walked into the room? I had a baby named after me, for God's sake! That's got to be good for at least 200 for the volunteering and a minimum of 125 annually for the full one hundred years."

"Who do you think you were, Mother Teresa?" Al shot back, "I'll split the difference with you, and that's being generous."

We would go back and forth like this until we reached an agreement or EF got sick of listening to us argue and made the call for us.

"Sold!" EF would call out when either of those things happened, slapping the desk to signal that the case was closed and another had moved into the docket.

Proud moments never lasted long for me. The boastful winds would leave my sails and be replaced by squalls of embarrassment and shame when the next episode of bad behavior sprang to life.

"Whoa, you really stepped in it that time," Al whooped with glee at one point, "That's got to be at least a 435 karma koin charge for what you did during life, you bad boy, and another 92 annually for eighty-three years."

He had just watched the installment of me proposing to Clarice, a girl I dated shortly before launching Hair Apparent, in a fancy restaurant. She accepted and said I had made her the happiest woman on the planet. If only it had ended there. The next scene, unfortunately, featured me dropping her off at home and, the second the door closed behind her after she blew one last kiss to me over her shoulder, speed-dialing another woman I wanted to take skiing with me at a Salt Lake City resort the next weekend. She called back later and left a far too detailed message on my voice mail. How could I know that Clarice would figure out the password?

"Ahhh, she really wasn't all that interested in me, Al," I replied weakly, "Clarice would have moved on anyway. How about hitting me with a 200 karma koin charge for how I treated her and another 30 annually for twenty-seven years?"

"You cannot be serious. Clarice was so upset that she quit her job and is now living in a vegan commune out west. Look— she got them to name a compost heap after you."

Sure enough, Al brought up the image. Not only was it a large heap, but the link to me couldn't be disputed after Al zeroed in on a plaque in front of it that displayed my name, picture, and voice mail password. I jumped in my seat when EF's voice boomed out.

"Sold at Mr. Borland's original estimate."

And so it went as we sorted through the bad, the ugly, and, nowhere near often enough, the good. My greatest hits were few and never took long to play.

WHEN THE WHIP COMES DOWN

At the end of the last, long day EF directed us to a page near the end of our binders that instantly flashed onto the blackboard behind him.

THE GOOD
PRESENT VALUE OF KARMIC KONTRIBUTIONS
Blessing-Adjusted Discount:
Years Shined On:
Karma Koin Kontributions:
Present Value:

"Bear in mind, gentlemen, that the figures I am about to give you are the results of the work we produced during this past week's AOL, which stands for Audit of a Lifetime. A group of HAPs in training still need to verify the results and make any necessary adjustments. Then everything is sent in to the ER department—the Eternal Review—and after evaluation the HAPs either pass or fail. You, Luke, will shortly after be informed of your own passage, be it up or down. As this is a new process, there may be some kinks to work out along the way."

"So I'm just a guinea pig here, then?" I protested.

"I did hear that term bandied about frequently when those whose lives you touched were discussing you, though the 'guinea' part was generally left out," EF retorted. He paused for effect and continued on.

"The BAD rate—the Blessing-Adjusted Discount—used for the present value of future karma koin flows is 4 percent, based on the obvious deficits in the Adams operating system. We used the maximum of one hundred years permitted for a judgee in this category. Together these two factors served to maximize the value of the good done. Do you understand these facts as I have explained them?" EF asked me.

I told him I did, though this didn't mean I was anxious to see how the numbers played out.

"The average karma koin kontribution per year is calculated to be 637. After discounting, this yields a present value of 33,450 karma koins."

"At least that's something in the positive column," Al leaned over and whispered. I think he was trying to reassure me.

"That it is, Mr. Borland, and let us now examine the costs of Mr. Adams' life activities. Please turn to the next page in your binders."

We did, and this is what we saw. It also materialized behind EF on the blackboard.

THE BAD AND THE UGLY
PRESENT VALUE OF KARMIC KOSTS
BAD (Blessing-Adjusted Discount) Rate:
Years Darkened:
Karma Koins Killed Annually:
Present Value:

EF cleared his throat and resumed the lecture.

"In this we used the kindest, gentlest BAD rate that could reasonably be chosen, again with the rationale that we are evaluating a man with severely limited powers of insight. That rate is 24 percent."

The feeling of dread knotting up my insides loosened a bit, for I knew the high rate would give me a lower present value. The loosening stopped, then reversed itself, when EF began speaking again.

"Though the ill effects of your actions, Mr. Adams, will last more than one hundred years, we kept the hundred from the first chart in the name of the matching principle. Even still, the annual karma koin kost of your detrimental actions worked out to be 4,492 koins per year."

Next to me, Al whistled softly, as though his mind had already raced ahead and calculated the numbers before they became visible. EF stepped aside to give us an unobstructed view of the board.

"The result is before you," he said, with a sweep of his arm.

THE BAD AND THE UGLY
PRESENT VALUE OF KARMIC KOSTS

BAD (Blessing-Adjusted Discount) Rate:	24%
Years Darkened:	100

Karma Koins Killed Annually: 4,492
Present Value of Karmic Kosts: 41,319

Right away I knew this meant deep, deep trouble for me, as in a lower ring of Hell than I'd been sentenced to my first time through. How low would I go? What kind of despicable creatures would my neighbors be for eternity? If never-ending Justin Timberlake music was my initial punishment, what would I be tortured with this time—Milli Vanilli without the doctored vocals? The shock of it all kept me silent while EF finished his presentation.

"To conclude our calculations, let me introduce the final chart," EF announced, and the words were hardly out of his mouth when the chart materialized on the trusty blackboard.

INSTANT KARMA STRIKES
NET ETERNAL WORTH
Present Value of Karma Koins Kontributed to the Future:
Karma Koins Kontributed During Life:
Total Karmic Kontributions:
Present Value of Karma Koins Killed in the Future:
Karma Koins Killed During Life:
Total Karma Koin Killings:
Net Eternal Worth Deposited in Entirety After Life:

"All we are doing here is restating the present values and adding to them the lifetime karma koin numbers. These represent enhancements and divots, if you will. Our final figure is arrived at by subtracting karma koins killed from karma koins kontributed."

Al nudged me with his elbow.

"Hey, Luke, did you notice what you get from the first letters in the words of the bottom line?"

"No, Al, I'm too busy trying to remember where I put my flame-resistant underwear," I answered, feeling glummer with every word.

"Very observant, Mr. Borland," EF called out and clapped his hands together in delight. "The bottom line we arrive at is the NEW DEAL, and it is called such because it represents a bargain that has been struck on behalf of the Almighty."

"A bargain?" I shot back. "How can it be a bargain if I don't have a say in it?"

"But you did have your say, Mr. Adams; you had plenty of it, in fact. And until you become the Almighty, what is and is not a bargain lies beyond your power to understand or decide."

"This stinks to high heaven."

Urgently Al whispered to me, "Luke, for God's sake, don't argue with him. You'll aggravate him, and he might tack on more charges and all you will have accomplished is to dig yourself an even deeper hole."

"Well said, Mr. Borland," EF told him approvingly.

"And now, let us see just how deep the hole is."

This appeared as he spoke:

INSTANT KARMA STRIKES
NET ETERNAL WORTH

Present Value of Karma Koins Kontributed to the Future:	33,450
Karma Koins Kontributed During Life:	12,213
Total Karmic Kontributions:	44,663
Present Value of Karma Koins Killed in the Future:	41,319

Karma Koins Killed During Life:	19,212
Total Karma Koin Killings:	60,531
Net Eternal Worth Deposited in Entirety After Life:	(19,212)

A rare chortle came from EF. "Mr. Adams, the bottom line is that you will soon have to look up to see your original placement in Hell."

Hardly were the words out of his mouth before a new visitor to the classroom filled me with terror. My escort to Hell, the man mountain in white, strode through the door and stationed himself at EF's side.

I could not help but wonder aloud, "But what could be worse than an eternity of Justin Timberlake?"

My giant attendant put a finger the size of a hot dog on EF's sleeve and grinned at him. "You haven't told him about Justin's Christmas carols with Milli Vanilli, huh, boss?"

MISSION OF MERCY

Suddenly that tiny chair that had been chafing me so badly during my time in Purgatory felt like a good place to be. I pulled myself up from it and walked over to my escort, ready to get on whatever elevator he told me to, no matter how low the floor it was going to. In truth, the finding had not been a surprise and arguing about it seemed futile. But not, amazingly, to Al.

"Hold on there, Magilla," Al yelled out as the attendant escorted me toward the door, "We've overlooked something very important here."

EF's eyebrows rose in disbelief.

"Highly unlikely, Mr. Borland, but we have time, so please proceed to describe your imaginings."

"What's unlikely is that I'm going to bat for this guy after what he did to me, but the truth needs to be told if we're going to do this right. Besides, he'll probably still end up in Hell anyway."

"Al, please, I'm begging you, just get me raised up enough to be out of earshot of Justin and Milli Vanilli," I pleaded.

Al went to the nearest keyboard and typed a phrase into it. On the monitor flashed a scene from EternaTube of me with Esther and Javier just before I got in the cab and left for the airport.

"On his way to fleeing the country, Luke deeded his house and all the equipment in it to a couple who worked for him. By the time I returned from Brazil they were already on their way to making a fortune selling fake fur coats, which we saw and immediately switched over to. This could not have happened without Luke's gift."

EF stood there stroking his noble chin. To me it looked like his preference was to ignore these facts, let the decision stand, and be rid of me. His sense of divine duty must have won out. He shook his head ruefully as the wheels rolled to a decision.

"Here is what will happen, Mr. Borland and Mr. Adams. The two of you are to spend another two days, and not a second more, researching and reviewing whatever you can find of this incident and its future manifestations. Somehow it was overlooked. I doubt your final destination will change much, Mr. Adams, but in the name of accuracy, it is the right and proper thing to do."

EF turned to my escort. "You will be on call two days from now?"

"As always, sir."

Though we were in the habit of listening and believing when EF spoke, he was wrong this time. Our EternaTube research revealed that my gift was destined to keep on giving, generously, for many years to come. Not only did Esther and Javier take over the Hair Apparent location (their business was called Fur Now) and franchise their operations across the country; their success also enabled them to become American citizens. They had three beautiful children and lavished the best of everything on them. Their children grew up to be highly successful, generous members of their own communities. Fur Now went global and became a major employer and producer of quality, low-cost clothing.

The act of giving them the house and equipment was of no great value because I had no plans to come back. But what resulted from it, particularly their being able to use the equipment and my processes, came to a surprisingly large amount. Being very careful to use reasonable estimates that EF couldn't shoot down, we recalculated my NEW DEAL bottom line.

INSTANT KARMA STRIKES AGAIN
NET ETERNAL WORTH

Present Value of Karma Koins Kontributed to the Future:	47,084
Karma Koins Kontributed During Life:	13,916
Total Karmic Kontributions:	61,000
Present Value of Karma Koins Killed in the Future:	41,319
Karma Koins Killed During Life:	19,212
Total Karma Koin Killings:	60,531
Net Eternal Worth Deposited in Entirety After Life:	469

EF glared hard at the new result. We wouldn't have been surprised to see smoke coming out of his ears as his high-powered intelligence scoured our work for errors. Given his heavenly connections, it is surprising that he didn't make a plea to have the future altered.

Looking like he had just agreed to eat a week-old bucket of chum, EF turned to me and said, "Well, well, will wonders never cease. The negative score has been transformed to a positive. A very small positive, to be sure, when placed in the context of a life and beyond, but positive nonetheless. I did not think it possible, Mr. Adams, but you are going to Heaven."

When he saw the smile break across my face as I high-fived Al, EF shook his head in disgust and added, "Do not become too elated, sir, for the place set for you is at Heaven's lowest rung, much like a corporate career spent working in the basement mailroom with no hope of promotion."

"One question," I retorted, "Do Justin and Milli Vanilli play there?"

"Not unless you want them to."

"Then it is Heaven enough for me."

Eighteen

CLOSING TIME

We'll make great pets.

According to EF, all that remained to be done was for a team of HAPs in training—a HIT squad, as they were known—to audit our work. This was the applied part of their certification examination, and they would submit a report to an AudiTrix senior partner. The partner would review the results and issue an opinion letter attesting to their accuracy. This document was known as an Opinion Hereby Given On Destination, or OH GOD, and would itself be reviewed by a celestial committee. If accepted, it would become my ticket to paradise, which even the lowest spot in Heaven looked like in comparison to where I had thought I was headed.

AND ALL SHALL BE REVEALED

EF appeared much more relaxed than I had seen him so far, so I took the opportunity to ask him a question.

"EF, in all the excitement around the viewing and calculating, I never did become clear on what role the book I'm working on is going to play. Originally I was told it would be the thing that decided where I went."

"A fair question, Mr. Adams. The intent was never to have you write a training manual based on your experiences. Instead, the act of writing made you examine and delve into your life, and you gained a much deeper understanding of yourself in the process, no?"

"That I surely did."

EF nodded in approval. "What the living do not realize is their places in Heaven or Hell are not permanent homes but rather starting points. By giving you the opportunity to come to terms with yourself, you enter Heaven much better equipped to advance."

"So I'm not stuck in the mailroom forever?"

"Well, you will be if you get lazy. It is, as you pointed out, a far better location than where it appeared you were headed."

"So everybody has to write a book on accounting after they die?" I asked doubtfully.

"No, most people would rather just go to Hell than do that," EF answered with a laugh. "The idea is to take the thing a person used most abusively in life and create something new with it that is positive."

"Kind of like having a chance to generate new revenue to make up for an old expense?"

"Exactly. You see, your wisdom is growing already. You can think of the Heaven you barely eked your way into as a new phase of much more challenging operations."

"Does that mean AudiTrix doesn't use any accounting in the judgment process?"

"No, it does, for all of the reasons you have described so far. In your case, this proves to be a benefit, because your area of spectacular sin happens to be in an area where those going through the judgment need enlightenment, so it really will be used as a guide if it is good enough. The good news here, which should be a wonderful motivator as you finish up, is that each time it proves useful to another person, you will receive a little bump up in status. The effect will be minimal per individual, but if you help a lot of people you will definitely experience a promotion."

"So what I am writing serves as both a preview and an explanation?"

"If you do a good job, that is correct. You see, it could have a significant impact on the NEW DEAL bottom-line score. The quality of understanding and insight shown and developed is taken into account when deciding on time periods and discount rates, and you have seen how these can tilt the ending balance one way or the other."

"I sure have."

Al chimed in now from his seat in front of a monitor. He had already regressed to giggling at clips he kept finding from my younger years by typing in creative search terms. "So having gone through all this, not to mention my pulling his butt from the fire, will give me an advantage when I begin my own process?"

"Sure," I cut in, "and every time you laugh at me, another pile of karma koins is deducted from your account."

Before Al could respond, EF cut in. "Do not worry, Mr. Borland, those clips are already making the rounds and are sure to become eternal hits. And in answer to your question, your experience has propelled you well along a positive learning curve, so you indeed will begin the proceedings from a position of strength."

I had a rare sensible thought and shared it immediately.

"You know, if judgees have the chance to improve their understanding of themselves after death, wouldn't it make sense to run a similar process during life?"

"Certainly, Mr. Adams, that is what religions, philosophies, morals, values, laws, standards, and social institutions are for. But having humans pause in the midst of living their lives to conduct a strategic audit may indeed be a good idea."

It pleased me to have come up with a suggestion that EF took seriously. Who knew, maybe it would be implemented some day. Before I could bask in my glow for too long, though, EF gave me something new to worry about.

CLOSING TIME

"Speaking of achieving an understanding of themselves, that is a human shortcoming AudiTrix and He Who Hired Them are increasingly concerned about."

"What do you mean?" I asked.

"With their lack of self-knowledge, humans have quite a history of acting first and thinking rationally much later, if at all. It is only through self-interest that they can get along at all, so weak is the human commitment to doing what is right on its own merits. This limits the value of their overall contribution."

EF went on to tell me that the next morning the HAPs in training would go through a seminar where they would learn how to close individual NEW DEAL scores, mine in particular, and transfer them to Earth's books. Earth's new bottom line, then, would be closed into the Universal Set of Books.

"Depending on the results," EF added, "you may be witness to a very interesting discussion."

"About what?"

"About whether Earth is to continue as a going concern."

"Huh?" was all I could manage.

"From the beginning, Earth has been an underperforming entity whose results only recently began coming close to the break-even point. As part of the AudiTrix mission, planets deemed to have meager prospects are to be culled from the constellation of operating sites."

"But what would happen to the billions of people living on Earth?" I asked, aghast.

EF held his hands up to reassure me. "Don't worry, should the planet be taken offline, earthlings will be given new homes at locations throughout the universe."

"And what would they do there?"

"Pets—humans make great pets."

EF cut loose with a hearty laugh at the stricken look on my face.

"Don't worry, my boy. The decision is not to be made for a while yet. Humans as pets was my idea, but the more I see of human behavior, the more I doubt the species is trainable enough."

The HAPs arrived the next morning and met in a different part of the building. They didn't have any questions for me and I never laid eyes on them. The closest I came was getting a look at the closing entries they made, pending final approval. EF called me into the classroom where they were reproduced on the board.

SPARE CHANGE

Adams NEW DEAL

equity	469	
Earth's Equity		469

To record the closing of the Luke Adams' equity account and transfer to Earth's account

"Well, Mr. Adams, this is what you have been waiting for. The HAPs approved our figures. Your account is now closed and the net equity added to Earth's."

"Will the positive equity put Earth in a better position?" I asked.

"To be honest, sir, this is an unusually small contribution. For perspective, consider the net equity added after Norman Borlaug died. It was in the billions of karma koins," EF sniffed.

I didn't want to look stupid by admitting I had no idea who Borlaug was, but I think EF knew. Instead, I asked, "So what happens now?"

"For that I defer to my assistant. Good-bye, Mr. Adams. I wish you well."

With that, EF shook my hand quickly and strode out of the room. Immediately the man mountain attendant in white came in.

"How did you do that without trampling EF?" I asked.

He looked at me like it was the dumbest question ever asked.

"You think the man goes around in that form everywhere?"

I decided to leave that one alone for now.

"Okay, then, I'm ready for my last elevator ride. I'm going up this time," I told him with pride.

"Don't get too excited," my giant friend answered. "It'll be such a short trip you could make it with a step stool."

He laughed at his own joke all the way through the labyrinth of corridors that took us to the elevators. After the doors opened and the attendant stepped through, I tried to follow and stand in the small space that remained for me. Suddenly everything became blurry. I felt like I was beginning to faint and staggered backward.

"Hey, I'm already dead, I shouldn't be passing out. What's going on?" I asked weakly.

"Looks to me like you're about to have an in-body experience. Catch you on the other side."

The elevator doors closed as I collapsed to the floor.

Nineteen

PASSAGE OF THE PRODIGAL SON

Never give up hope, for even the prodigal son saved himself.

The next thing I knew I was in the middle of a nightmare that featured EF walking me on a leash in a park filled with other owners doing the same with their pets, humans of all shapes, sizes, and ages. Everywhere I looked were signs saying "Please curb your human."

"No, no," I groaned, "I'm not supposed to be a pet. I'm already dead, I'm already dead."

"Mr. Adams, you have finally awakened, let me go get the doctor," said a voice from above my head.

I opened my eyes and saw a pretty Brazilian nurse turning to hurry out of the room.

"Wait, miss, wait," I cried out feverishly. "You weren't made into a pet—how did you escape?"

"Mr. Adams, there are no such things as human pets."

"Yes, oh yes there are, just look at my leash," I insisted, and brandished it as proof.

She hurried over and gently but firmly took hold of my arm and lowered it.

"That is a catheter, and if you pull it out, you will be in terrible pain."

As my head cleared, I took in my surroundings. I was on my back in a private hospital room.

"How did I get here? I was supposed to be on my way to Heaven."

"You mean a heaven for pets?" she asked, and then added, "Are you on any psychiatric meds?"

"No, but maybe I should be." I motioned at the room around me. "This makes no sense."

"It is not uncommon for victims of head trauma to feel that way," she told me in her professionally sympathetic voice.

"I didn't suffer any trauma. I just got dizzy and fainted when I tried to get on an elevator."

"Mr. Adams, you must have the order of events mixed up, and that is not surprising considering that you have been unconscious for three days. In fact, the fishermen who brought you here thought you were already dead."

"Three days! You can't be serious."

"What happened to you is very serious and has impacted your memory. The wing of your hang-glider broke off and you flew into the ocean. A fishing trawler picked you up in its net, and you had a Box jellyfish stuck on top of your head. Do you remember any of that?" she asked.

"Sure, but that happened longer than three days ago, I think, and what is a Box jellyfish? I thought they were all the same."

"Oh no, I used to live in Australia and there were lots of them in the ocean there. Box jellyfish have one of the most lethal stings of any animal there is. A big one was stuck to your head and covered most of your face. When you came in, your head was swelled up like a beach ball."

I reached up and felt the contours of my face. It seemed to be the normal size, but it was covered with bumps, as though I had stuck my head into a beehive. Continuing upward, my hand discovered a head swathed in bandaging.

The nurse saw the question in my eyes and continued. "Unfortunately, when you fell out of the net with that thing on you, one of the fisherman thought you were a sea monster and hit you over the head with a club, and that is why you have been unconscious for so long. You are lucky not to have suffered a skull fracture."

"So I'm okay?"

"We still have to see what your mental functioning is like, but it appears so. Now, let me go get the doctor; she can tell you more," she finished and started to walk away. The nurse was through the door when she stopped and turned back toward me. "I almost forgot—you had a visitor yesterday. He looked like an actor in a television commercial, or maybe a series I remember from when I was a child, but I can't place him. He only stayed a few moments and left a letter for you on the night table."

After the nurse left, I looked over and spotted a folded piece of parchment held in place with a wax seal. I opened it and, sure enough, found a note written in EF's precise cursive.

Dear Mr. Adams,

The closing entries made by the heavenly auditing professionals were rejected by the oversight committee. In their opinion letter it was stated that it is policy not to accept equity amounts so small as to be neglible. They recommend that you be returned to Earth in the hope that what you have learned will enable you to build a more substantial equity balance. I decided to return you to Brazil at the site of your death. It was Mr. Borland's idea to have the fisherman club you. A nice flourish.

I advise you to return home and make amends for your crimes. I will see you again upon your next termination and expect to calculate a much higher NEW DEAL score.

Yours in Faith,
EF

P.S. Below is the journal entry reestablishing your earthly account. The balance is almost enough to buy a cup of coffee in Heaven.

Earth's Equity	469	
Adams' NEW DEAL Equity		469

To reestablish the Adams' equity account

Amazing. After everything I had been through, I was heading back to what I had run from. I would have to wrestle with the huge debts I owed. Hair Apparent, the venture that looked like it would be an unending gusher of money, had now been transformed into the fake fur business, which I knew nothing about. All looked hopeless and I felt lost. I didn't want to go back, but further flight did not appear to be a better option.

On second thought, I mused, as my head cleared and I got used to my surroundings, maybe everything following the hanggliding accident had merely been a dream and I could go right on with my permanent vacation after I recovered.

"I knew it would not take long before you started scheming again," said a youthful version of a familiar voice. I looked up and saw what looked like a blond, twenty-one-year-old surfer dude standing in the doorway.

"Come again?"

"You heard me, Mr. Adams."

The voice had quickly aged and I knew it instantly.

"Are you EF's son? You sound just like him."

"I am him. It has been three hundred years since I inhabited a human form on Earth, and it has been decreed that I become reacquainted with field work for my next assignment."

"And that assignment brings you here?"

"It brings me here to retrieve you to accompany me. Do you remember my mentioning the possibility of Earth's underperforming operations being discontinued?"

"Yes, now that I think about it, I do."

"AudiTrix has charged me with a task and requested that you assist me. Since we are both on Earth already, the mission begins tomorrow."

"And what is the mission, exactly?" I asked, wondering if it would prove to be an upgrade or a downgrade from my currently dismal trajectory.

"It is our job to ascertain if humans are making sufficient progress in their ability to handle risk to retain Earth as a going concern."

"But haven't we made good progress?"

"Certainly, in the number of countries with the capacity to commit nuclear genocide. How do you account for that?"

"I don't know."

"Then rise from your deathbed and let us get to work!"

ACKNOWLEDGMENTS

Thanks to Tom Dunne and the editorial staff at Thomas Dunne Books for their time, tolerance, and improvements. The idea for karma koins came from my sister, Janice Hovey, who generates lots of good karma every day. Thanks!

While this book was in process I took a break so that super-surgeon Dr. Michael Argenziano, of Columbia Presbyterian Hospital, could perform a bionic mitral valve repair. It left me feeling better than ever and boosted the blood flow to my brain—a badly needed upgrade I am very grateful for.

Speaking of upgrades, I thank Coach Dom, a great guy in a tough business, of Roc Boxing and Fitness for showing me a better and more creative approach to good health.